Respect Matters

Real life scenarios provide powerful discussion starters for all aspects of respect

R.E. Myers

A
GOOD
YEAR
BOOK™

Dedication

For my son, Hal, with much love and admiration.

Good Year Books

Are available for most basic curriculum subjects plus many enrichment areas. For more Good Year Books, contact your local bookseller or educational dealer. For a complete catalog with information about other Good Year Books, please contact:

Good Year Books
P.O. Box 91858
Tucson, AZ 85752-1858
www.goodyearbooks.com

Cover design: Gary Smith, Performance Design
Text design: Doug Goewey
Drawings: Sean O'Neill
Cover photos: comstock.com

ISBN-10: 1-59647-056-9
ISBN-13: 978-1-59647-056-9
1 2 3 4 5 6 7 8 9 10 – DBH – 09 08 07 06 05

Contents

Contents

Introduction

We're at a point in the history of American education where opinions are almost equally divided as to whether the schools should attempt to deal with the character and attitudes of students or redouble efforts to teach fundamental skills. From the days of the McGuffey readers, when moral lessons were the subject matter of reading instruction, we've arrived at a time when lessons in moral education and social and emotional learning are again being offered as panaceas for our pervasive social problems. Should teachers attempt to *teach* their students morals, or even the basics of civil behavior? This book represents one small answer in the affirmative.

You *can* expose young people to certain concepts and precepts when engaging them in dialogues about appropriate and inappropriate behavior of both adults and juveniles. Educators who are currently trying to integrate lessons in social and emotional learning have proved that, as was the case with the McGuffey readers, the instructions can be located in the regular curriculum, but it can be infused with matters that affect students now—with such topics as crime, alienation, divorce, teenage pregnancy, war, responsibility, and respect (Elias, Bruene-Butler, Blum, and Schuyler, 1997).

Why should the schools be concerned with social and emotional education? There are at least three powerful reasons. The first one is obvious—namely, so that schools can be safe, healthy places for students, teachers, and staff. The sooner in their lives that young people come to grips with a sense of responsibility for their own behavior, the sooner police will no longer be patrolling the halls of junior and senior high schools. Second, we must teach social education because teachers, more and more, have become surrogate parents. There has to be a sufficient number of admirable adult models that children can emulate. The third reason is that our society as a whole has become one that needs revitalization of its civic imperatives. We can't ignore the accumulating evidence that our moral and spiritual values are steadily eroding.

Respect Matters is an attempt to bring to the attention of students and teachers the fact that respect is the foundation for all civil behavior. There can be no civility—or morality—without respect. If we don't respect another person's worth, body, property, or privacy, we have destroyed the basis upon which citizens can exist amicably in a community. These serious topics are brought forth in the stories in *Respect Matters*.

Respect is a positive regard for the worth of someone or something. The concept includes respect for the rights and dignity of other people, for laws and authority, for nature, and for oneself. Respect connotes appreciation, understanding, and esteem. It is the indispensable element in positive relationships among individuals and groups of individuals.

All over the country young people are striving to inculcate genuine respect in their peers. Some examples are the Kids Committee in Albuquerque, New Mexico; People are People at Hoffman Estate High School in Hoffman Estates, Illinois; Teenagers Against Racial Prejudice in Reno, Nevada; CityKids Foundation in New York City, New York; and New Moon Publishers, an editorial board of eight- to fourteen-year-olds in, Duluth, Minnesota. Because of their awareness of problems of hatred, prejudice, and intolerance, it is the young people themselves who are acting.

There are several ways in which this collection of stories and activities can be used in the classroom. Perhaps foremost among them is an open discussion of the story, followed by students proposing practical strategies for solving the problem that is presented. When you administer a story's activity after the discussion, you give students an opportunity to examine in depth the type of respect that was illustrated in the story. Another way of using a story is to integrate it with a social studies, science, language arts, or science lesson. Some of the units fit nicely into curricular programs. For example, "Saplings and Cans" can fit into units about ecology, conservation, and biology, and "Billy the Bully" dovetails with units concerning mental health and citizenship. Most, if not all, of the stories and activities in this book can be integrated into the regular curriculum.

In the world of today's youth, "dissing" is a behavior that means disrespecting and insulting a youngster. If the idea of disrespect is so explosive in juvenile society, perhaps *respect* can be as powerful in defusing conflict and building good will.

Sources for Further Reading

Duvall, L. *Respecting Our Differences*. Minneapolis: Free Spirit Publishing, 1994.

Elias, M. J.; L. Bruene-Butler; L. Blum; and T. Schuyler. "How to Launch a Social and Emotional Learning Program." *Educational Leadership* 54 (1997): 15–19.

Goodlad, J. *A Place Called School*. New York: McGraw-Hill, 1984.

Lickona, T. *Educating for Character: How Our Schools Can Teach Respect and Responsibility*. New York: Bantam Books, 1991.

Myers, R. E. *Character Matters*. Glenview, IL: Good Year Books, 1999.

Rochester, J. M. *Class Warfare*. San Francisco: Encounter Books, 2002.

How to Use This Book

Each of this book's 25 units includes a story followed by several discussion questions and an activity. The questions include space for student responses. The story and questions are formatted so that you can duplicate them and hand them out to students. The next section of each unit is teacher material, which includes summary remarks about the story and information about the question responses, along with a student activity. Some activities include a handout page for students.

Note that you do not need to present the units in any particular order. Use them in whatever order is appropriate for your students.

The Right Way

The eight members of the Dance Club could not agree on the criteria for electing officers for the next year. Some wanted to elect the best dancer as the next president. There was little debate about who that was—Tom was everyone's choice. On the other hand, several members wanted the president to be the best organizer and leader, and that was obviously Ashley. She had been class president last year and had done an outstanding job. Still others wanted to elect someone as president who would "look good at the annual dance and be an excellent master of ceremonies"; that person was probably Ryan, who had even been a soloist for the school chorus. The debate rolled on.

When the discussion finally simmered down, it was obvious that every member of the club had some outstanding quality that might recommend her or him as a good president. Gradually, all of the members recognized that each of them had been mentioned as a possible president, and so a calm settled over the group.

"You know," began Marcus, "we must be a pretty special group. I think all of us have been mentioned as someone who could be president."

"That's what I like about this bunch—people are honest and don't just nominate their buddies," added Matt. "Each of us has something to offer, and we all recognize those things. Let's stop the discussion now and take a secret ballot. The one who gets the most votes is president."

RESPONSES

_____   _____
Name   **Date**

The Right Way: Student Responses

Think about your answers to the following questions and write your response to each.

1. The Dance Club may be an unusual group of young people. They love to disagree, but they have learned to listen to one another. When is disagreeing a sign of disrespect?

_____

_____

_____

_____

2. By the end of the school year, the Dance Club members seemed to have learned how to listen to each other and to even conduct productive meetings. Describe the kind of respect that they demonstrated for one another.

_____

_____

_____

_____

3. Do you think dancers tend to be more cooperative and more sensitive to others because they have to pay close attention to what their partners are doing? Explain.

_____

_____

_____

_____

The Right Way:
Respect for the Ideas of Others

The Story

It is just possible that a group of young people could behave in the way the Dance Club members did. Actually, we've seen one or two. Perhaps a discussion such as this one goes better without an adult present. That happens, too.

Listening is an art that has to be practiced continually. Just when you consider yourself a decent listener, you catch yourself interrupting or not listening because you're just waiting to jump in with a thought of your own. It doesn't work to feign interest when you're bored, either; you have to engage yourself mentally with the ideas expressed by others. By listening attentively to another person, you are giving respect to that person's ideas, concerns, and/or experiences.

The Questions

The first question is a bit tricky: when is disagreeing a sign of disrespect? Your students are old enough to know that there are people who enjoy disagreeing with others just for fun, or out of a bad habit, and those people aren't being disrespectful intentionally—it's just their way. On the other hand, there are quarrelsome and contentious people who seem to appreciate no one's ideas but their own—they're being disrespectful. In an earlier time it was believed that children were disrespectful of adults when they disagreed openly with the adults. Generally speaking, nowadays children are allowed to disagree and it's not regarded as a form of disrespect.

The second question asks for a description of the interactions of the Dance Club members. The point we want to make is that the ten members have learned to interact in generally polite and orderly ways.

We are only half-serious about the third question, but it is possible that paying a good deal of attention to a dancing partner's movements makes a dancer a more sympathetic and sensitive conversationalist. We haven't heard the hypothesis advanced anywhere, however.

A Listening Activity

You might conduct a follow-up activity that is in the nature of a checkup. Have your students review these listening principles after their discussion about "The Right Way." Then have them rate themselves (a scale of 1–10 will do) as to how well they observed each of these principles during that discussion. Because you won't have presented the listening principles before the discussion, they shouldn't feel embarrassed by scoring poorly on them.

Here are the principles:

1. Anticipate what the speaker will say. Whether you guess wrong or right, you'll remember better.

2. Concentrate on the speaker's message, not on his facial expressions, clothes, or mannerisms.

3. If the speaker makes several points, try to relate them in some way; that is, organize what the speaker says so that it makes sense to you.

4. Keep a clear head. Disregard language that triggers emotions or "pushes your buttons." It is the listener's task to filter out words that are meant to distract or inflame him or her.

5. Try to grasp the essence, or main idea, of what the speaker is saying.

6. Try to determine the speaker's purpose or motive in speaking.

7. Compare what the speaker says with what you know of the subject or what others have said about the subject.

We suggest that each student evaluate himself or herself independently. After your students have evaluated their own listening skills, you might want to try a listening activity. One, "The Automatic Chairman," has been effective with young people of all ages in helping them listen to another's point of view with a relatively receptive mind. The "Chairman" is not human and is not really automatic; "he" might better be described as *circulating*. Any object that can be easily handed from one individual to another can serve as the Chairman. (Once, in a pinch, we used a long-necked vase.)

The members of a group are seated in a circle to discuss a topic of vital interest; the technique works best if the topic is controversial or of genuine concern to the individuals who are participating. You may choose to be a member of the group, or you may be an observer who is available to interpret the few rules if the occasion arises.

The Chairman, which is placed in front of someone, entitles the person to speak about the topic under discussion. No one may interrupt the speaker while the Chairman is in front of him or her. When the speaker is finished, he or she passes the Chairman to the next person in a clockwise direction. Other participants may want to jot down notes when someone is talking in order to remember points they wish to make when the Chairman reaches them.

After the Chairman has made at least one round trip, he may be passed directly to any participant who wishes to contribute to the discussion at that time. No one is obliged to speak, however. If the Chairman is placed in front of someone who doesn't wish to contribute at that moment, he is simply passed to the next person.

When students abide by these few rules, they report that they learn more from their class discussion because they attend to the arguments of others instead of continually thinking of retorts. No one really is able to listen and to build a case of her or his own simultaneously. Another important result is that the few individuals who usually dominate any class discussion are unable to do so when the Automatic Chairman "leads" a discussion. Some students report that for the first time they have felt free to speak up in these sessions.

Mangroves

Some students thought that Ms. Jenkins was a bit wacky about poetry. Here it was the second week of October and she hadn't talked about much else to her English class. To her chagrin, however, Ms. Jenkins was finding that some of her students had no enthusiasm for poetry. One Saturday, when she was working on a bulletin board in her classroom featuring Robert Frost, two boys were passing her room. The door was closed but the transom above it was open.

"What is it with her anyway?" one of the boys asked.

"Oh, I don't know . . . she's bonkers about poetry," said the second boy. "Can't see it myself."

"I'm with you," remarked the first boy.

Ms. Jenkins couldn't quite identify the voices, but she thought they sounded like Marcus and Ryan. Well, Ms. Jenkins wasn't discouraged.

What if a couple of students were disenchanted with poetry? Boys their age usually were. She'd go right ahead and urge her students to submit their poems for the countywide contest. Some of them were writing very interesting poetry. Ms. Jenkins was expecting more promising verses on Monday, when an assignment requiring an original poem was due.

Ms. Jenkins was more than pleased with several of the poems turned in, especially Matt's poem about mangroves. On Wednesday she approached Matt at the beginning of the period. "Matt, would you like to submit your poem about mangroves, along with some others by your classmates, in the contest?"

"No, I don't think so," Matt answered.

Ms. Jenkins was puzzled because she thought Matt's poem was an especially picturesque one, and she thought it had a chance of winning a prize. Later on, just before the deadline for sending in entries, Ms. Jenkins asked for Matt's permission to include his poem with the others being submitted.

"Have your changed your mind, Matt?" she asked him at the end of class.

"No," he grunted.

That was that. Ms. Jenkins didn't give it much more thought for a month or so. Then she spotted a familiar verse in an anthology of poetry. It was about mangroves.

Name   **Date**

Mangroves: Student Responses

Think about your answers to the following questions and write your response to each.

1. Why would Matt take a published poem and turn it in as his own for an assignment?

_____

_____

_____

_____

2. Was Ms. Jenkins naive in thinking Matt could write such a good poem? Why do you think so?

_____

_____

_____

_____

3. There is a word for taking someone else's writing and passing it off as your own. What is it?

_____

4. Besides being dishonest, Matt was also showing disrespect for at least two people. Who were they?

_____

For the Teacher

Mangroves:
Respect for Intellectual Property of Others

The Story

You may have had an experience similar to that of Ms. Jenkins's. There is a temptation to plagiarize poems, essays, and reports that begins in elementary school and goes through graduate school and beyond. In recent times, two prominent leaders of our society have been caught plagiarizing material for a scholarly work and for a speech. Although the teacher's name was not Ms. Jenkins, this story is quite true.

The Questions

Some young people feel a strong pressure to hand in a piece of writing that will get them a good grade. The reasons for plagiarizing a poem or an essay are the same as for other kinds of cheating. The more pressure, the more cheating—witness the periodic scandals in the service academies. Moreover, some youngsters have a very difficult time writing an original composition. They aren't as threatened when asked to write a report after they have gathered facts, but when they are asked to produce something that comes only from their imaginations, they are genuinely scared.

Plagiarists figure that the odds are in their favor. The professor won't remember that essay residing in the fraternity's file written ten years ago. Ms. Jenkins can't have read all the poetry published in the last three or four decades. We once had an audacious young student turn in the recently published *The Cat in the Hat*, thinking that it was the kind of material a seventh-grade English teacher was unlikely to read. She was right. We didn't run into it for a couple of years when we began to read to our first-born child. On the other hand, our second-born was upset when a poem she had written when she was nine was rejected by her sixth-grade teacher as being obviously too well written to be a child's.

The word to describe Matt's act, of course, is plagiarism. Some of your students might know it. We hope that none practice it.

Actually, Matt was showing disrespect for three persons—Ms. Jenkins, the author of the published poem, and himself.

An Activity about Plagiarism and Attribution

A natural outcome of a discussion of plagiarism is a lesson about attribution. Elementary school students are prone to copy from the encyclopedia, and now that encyclopedias are available on home computers, the problem is exacerbated. Students in middle school and high school are also careless about attributing the sources of their ideas in reports, compositions, and other assignments.

Some teachers make it a point to be sure that their students know the difference between an indirect quotation and plagiarism. The line between the two is often blurred. Moreover, many students seem completely unacquainted with quotation marks. We're doing these young people a disservice if we don't point out the necessity of being intellectually honest and giving credit to the writers whose ideas we use. As an example, you might remember that newspapers and television news programs around the country recently carried the story of a second Boston columnist who had been fired by his newspaper for plagiarism, following a colleague who was dismissed for the same offense a few weeks earlier.

Give your students a copy of the handout on pages 14–15. Ask them to respond with a **T** for "true" or **F** for "false" to each question. Follow up with a group discussion of their responses to ensure that they understand the rules of attribution.

Activity Answers

1. **T**

2. **T**

3. **T**

4. **T**. In formal writing, ideas that come from a definite source should be given attribution. It isn't necessary in informal writing if it is just a general idea.

5. **T**

6. It depends upon how closely the ideas are to those of the seeker or writer. Generally speaking, it is courteous and more correct to give credit.

7. **T**

8. **T**. The key word here is *publish*. If it isn't published, as it wouldn't be for a school assignment, there is no violation of copyright.

9. **T**. As long as the copy is not circulated for profit, which it probably wouldn't be in a school report or other paper, it is all right—but give credit to the artist.

10. **T** for schoolwork, but not for publications that are sold for profit. In those cases, there must be permission from the publisher and a fee may be required.

ACTIVITY

Name _____   **Date** _____

Mangroves: An Activity about Plagiarism and Attribution

Attribution

Place a **T** to the left of each statement if you think it is true and an **F** if you think it is false.

_____ **1.** In a report or term paper, when you quote, word-for-word, someone's words, you must enclose them with quotation marks.

_____ **2.** When you paraphrase someone's words, either spoken or written, it isn't necessary to use quotation marks.

_____ **3.** When you paraphrase someone's words, either spoken or written, it is proper to give the person you are paraphrasing credit for his or her ideas.

_____ **4.** If you get the general idea from an article in an encyclopedia, it isn't necessary to reveal the source of your writing.

Name   Date

_____ **5.** If you use material from a book, article, or other source, it is proper and right to cite the source in the body of your writing or in the bibliography or in a footnote.

_____ **6.** If you modify someone's ideas and make them a little different from those of the speaker or author, it isn't necessary to give the speaker or writer credit.

_____ **7.** If you copy a cartoon or drawing, it is necessary to give credit to the illustrator, even if you change a feature of the cartoon or drawing.

_____ **8.** If you copy and publish a cartoon or drawing without permission from the illustrator, you are probably violating a copyright. You must determine whether the cartoon or drawing is copyrighted before you publish a version of it.

_____ **9.** It is all right to copy a cartoon or drawing in a report or other paper to be handed in at school without asking for the illustrator's permission.

_____ **10.** It is all right to quote a long section of an article (more than a page long) in a paper as long as you note the source.

Tom's Job

When his last class was dismissed on Fridays, Tom went directly to a retirement residence about a mile from school. He rode his bike to the large three-story building and parked it in the back near some redwood trees. Tom had been working as a server at the retirement residence for the past two months. He was the youngest employee of the company that owned and operated the residence. Tom got the job after a friend who worked in the dining room told him that they desperately needed a server when two servers suddenly called in sick. He liked the job, and he was able to save some money so he could update his computer.

Tom got a great deal of satisfaction from the job because he was courteous to the residents and they liked him. Sometimes they kidded him, and he joked back with them—but in a polite way. He genuinely liked older people. In fact, two of his favorite people in the whole world were his grandmother and grandfather. They lived in the same neighborhood in which Tom and his family lived, and he saw them two or three times a week.

As usual, Tom was right on time in reporting to the head cook in the kitchen one Friday. He put on his jacket and tie and began setting up the tables with napkins, silverware, and glasses. While he was busy at the tables, Duffy, one of the older residents, came up to him.

"Hello, Tom. I wonder if I could ask you a favor?" said Duffy.

"Certainly," Tom responded. "What can I do to help you?"

"There is a small shelf I want to put up in my apartment, and I'm afraid I no longer am steady enough to fasten it properly," said Duffy.

"Sure. When I'm through with my serving, I can go right to your apartment and put it up," Tom offered.

True to his word, at the conclusion of the meal Tom went to Duffy's table and got the key to his apartment. In only six or seven minutes, he was able to put up the shelf where Duffy had told him to put it.

On the next Friday, Duffy again approached Tom as he was putting silverware and napkins on the tables.

"You did a fine job with that shelf, Tom. Here . . . I want to pay you for your trouble."

"Oh, no, thank you," Tom replied. "I couldn't accept any money for that. It didn't take any time at all—just a few minutes. I was happy to help you."

"Please, Tom. I'd feel better if you'd take this," Duffy said, extending a ten-dollar bill in his hand to Tom.

"Thanks, anyway," Tom smiled. "Anytime I can help you or anyone here, I'm happy to do so."

RESPONSES

_____   _____
              Name   **Date**

Tom's Job: Student Responses

Think about your answers to the following questions and write your
response to each.

1. Some servers at the residence did accept money from the residents
for odd jobs. Was Tom foolish to refuse Duffy's money? Why or why not?

_____

_____

_____

_____

2. Do you feel uncomfortable around older people? If so, why do you
feel uncomfortable with them?

_____

_____

_____

_____

3. How do you get along with people who are sixty or older?

_____

_____

_____

_____

4. What do you suppose Tom likes about older people?

_____

_____

_____

_____

Tom's Job:
Respect for Older People

The Story

Essentially, the story about Tom and his job at the retirement residence is true. He could sound too "goody-goody" to your students, even though there are many young people like him. Occasionally there are stories in the newspapers about teens who have gone out of their way to be helpful to senior citizens, and perhaps you will be able to refer to one if your students don't "buy" the story of Tom's admiration for and rapport with seniors.

The Questions

Depending upon their attitudes toward money and toward helping others, your students will either think Tom foolish or quite normal. Personal altruism isn't exactly a big problem in our society, although we make a big deal out of charitable giving.

If some of your students have had very little contact with senior citizens, they may well feel a little uncomfortable with them when encountering them for any time longer than thirty seconds. One of the finest efforts for fostering intergenerational understanding has been the program in which retired people work as aides in the schools. If your students have had such a program in their schools, they are quite lucky.

The third question is designed to elicit personal experiences from your students, and so you may want to have them write about those experiences before sharing them, if they wish, in a discussion. All of us have had encounters with cranky seniors, as well as those that are unfailingly friendly and kind. People's personality traits are supposed to become more pronounced in old age, and, if that is true, we should find the cantankerous growing more so. Unfortunately, some of those seniors are still acting as if young people are their natural enemies. It is also possible that the crabby ones will become much more mellow as they age.

Perhaps the most promising of the four questions in terms of insightful thinking is the one that asks your students to name the characteristics of seniors that Tom likes. The story doesn't provide many clues, and so we presume your students will call upon their own experiences with family members, church and community members, and friends in order to come up with a list of positive characteristics. Television features seniors intermittently, but in recent times several popular programs oriented toward an older audience have been dropped from the programming. That may be just as well with regard to this question because your students won't base their impressions on the scripted personalities of television characters.

For the Teacher

A Research Activity about Senior Citizens

There may be a retirement residence in your community, but if not there probably is one not too far away. As the U.S. population ages, more and more facilities are being created to accommodate retirees. It is possible that one or more of your students has had some contact with a retirement residence, and if that is so he or she can provide information about it. Finding out more about retirement residences, nursing homes, convalescent institutions, and foster homes for senior citizens would be a worthy activity for your students.

Long before *they* are ready to retire, your students will most likely be faced with the dilemma that a very large number of people are confronted with now, namely, what is the best way to care for my aged parents (and other relatives)? In all probability, the parents of some of your students are grappling with that problem right now. Asking your students to do some rudimentary research about this problem of caring for the aged and those with disabilities is one of the best assignments you can make to give them an understanding of what their future lives are going to be like.

Topics that they might investigate:

- What are the differences between retirement residences, nursing homes, and convalescent hospitals?

- What are the requirements for becoming a resident in a retirement residence? Are they for-profit or not-for-profit businesses? Are residents relatively happy in these places?

- Churches and fraternal organizations have had facilities for the aged and infirm for about as long as there has been a United States. Are they playing a less important role now in caring for the elderly, physically and mentally challenged, and those who are critically ill?

- There are retirement residences with medical facilities and personnel where, if you give them all of your money, you can be taken care of for the rest of your days. Are there more or fewer of this kind of retirement residence than there used to be? Are people who live a relatively short time cheated in these places?

This final question is a rather deep one. If you live the rest of your life with relatively little worry about medical care and in congenial surroundings, you have made a good bargain, regardless of how long you live. The question arises mostly in whether heirs or others would be cheated by your having given the institution all of your assets.

Completion

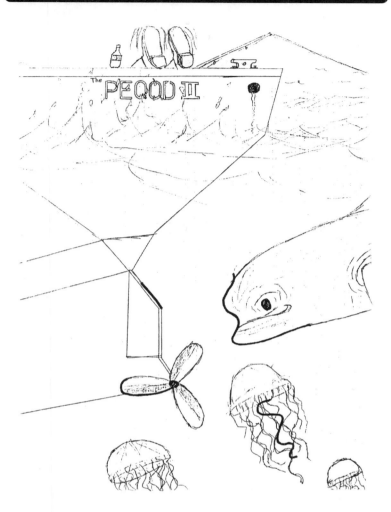

This drawing is what resulted when Norman's teacher decided that her class needed a change of pace one warm afternoon in May. She thought that they should get away from reading, reciting, and writing for a little while. Norman welcomed the opportunity to get away from the regular routine, especially because he enjoyed sketching and doodling.

A few of the students had a bit of trouble connecting the lines at first, and they looked around at what others were doing, but most of Norman's classmates followed the teacher's directions and picked up their pencils, crayons, and markers and started drawing.

After twenty minutes or so, Norman had finished his drawing. Miriam, who sat behind him, said: "I like that, Norman."

Tom's desk was to the side of Norman's, and when he heard Miriam's remark he looked over and said: "Yeah, that's good, Norman."

Norman wasn't sure that what he had done was so special, but he felt good about his classmates' approval of his drawing.

_____   _____
               Name   **Date**

Completion: Student Responses

Think about your answers to the following questions and write your response to each.

1. Can you see the original lines that Norman added to when he did his drawing?

_____

2. Do you think Tom and Miriam were just trying to be kind to Norman? Why do you think so?

_____

_____

_____

_____

3. Have you ever had a drawing exercise like this one? If so, did you enjoy it? Why or why not?

_____

_____

_____

_____

Completion:
Respect for Creative Efforts

The Story

There is no dramatic element in this little story. Norman responds to an incomplete figure such as those used in Torrance's Incomplete Figures Test, producing a drawing that is approved of by two of his classmates. Norman's complete drawing is shown on page 21. This is the type of drawing activity that hundreds of thousands of young people and adults have been challenged by in Torrance's tests of creative thinking. It has also been successful as a simple art activity.

The drawing in the unit was done by a talented thirteen-year-old boy who has a wide range of interests and a good sense of humor. There are ways of assessing the drawings of individuals who complete figures such as the one Norman dealt with. It is not appropriate, however, to go into ways of evaluating these productions when our point is simply that the creative ideas of individuals are worthy of respect. If the ideas are expressed honestly and in earnest, they are worthy of respect on the grounds that they reflect the individuality of the person.

The Questions

Any kind of self-expression raises troublesome questions about evaluation. People's tastes vary greatly, and consequently rarely is a group of individuals unanimous in praising a drawing, painting, dance, play, or song. Whether or not Norman's completed figure is artistic is not really under consideration. It is likely to appeal to the viewer if it is seen as clever in incorporating all of the original lines into a unified composition. It is even more likely to be appreciated if it is surprising.

If you or your students have actually been given one of Torrance's Incomplete Figures tests, this unit will be more meaningful than it might otherwise have been.

Reference

Torrance, E. P. *Torrance Tests of Creative Thinking*. Bensonville, IL: Scholastic Testing Service, 1990.

For the Teacher

A Drawing Activity Eliciting Creativity

This is a great follow-up activity and is identical to the one Norman did. Be sure to tell your students that it's fun, but make sure that they keep their drawings in good taste. This enables you to engage your students in a nonthreatening activity out of which they can find something positive in another person's efforts. Because creative efforts are personal, it takes a little courage to reveal oneself in an unself-conscious manner. Even people who don't like to draw don't mind connecting the lines because it's a little like doing a puzzle.

Distribute the handout on page 25. Then give your students these instructions:

"Here is another incomplete figure you can finish yourself. To give yourself ideas, rotate the figure 90° and then 180° and 270°. When you have added lines and color—and even bits of paper if you wish—and are satisfied with your picture, give it a title. Then, if you'd like, exchange your drawing with a friend. Let the friend know what you like about his or her drawing—its ideas, colors, shadings, humor, drama, title, or its message. You are sure to find something to like in what your friend has done."

Name   Date

Completion: An Activity Eliciting Creativity

What Is It?

Beginning with the lines below, see what kind of object you can draw. Use as many additional lines as you would like. When you have completed your drawing, you may wish to color it.

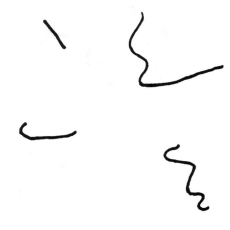

1.   What does this look like to you?

_____

_____

_____

2.   Make up a story that features your object in some way. Write your story on the back of this sheet of paper. Be sure to give your story a title.

Fish for Dinner

Tom spent a lot of time in the school library reading about various cultures throughout the world. His own heritage was Vietnamese. His father and mother had come to this country about twenty years ago after trying to emigrate from Vietnam for many years. On several occasions Tom had encountered David Goldstein at the library, and after awhile they became friends. David was very interested in history and in different cultures also.

One day, when Tom had spent some time talking with David before going to the Dance Club, he had an idea: He could invite David over for dinner. Tom knew that, first of all, he had better talk with his mother. Tom's mother was there when he came home from school, and he asked her about inviting David for dinner.

"I'm not sure about tonight, Tom. We're having a fish soup, and David's family may have some restrictions on their diet. He's Jewish, isn't he? I've heard that some Jewish people follow strict rules about what they can eat."

"I'll find out, Mama," said Tom. "Maybe we can have some food tomorrow that he's able to eat that we can all enjoy."

RESPONSES

Name

Date

Fish for Dinner: Student Responses

Think about your answers to the following questions and write your response to each.

1. Tom's mother was correct in saying that there are religious groups, including Orthodox Jews, who are strict in observing dietary laws. It happened that both of David's parents were Orthodox Jews. What might have happened if David came to dinner and all there was to eat was fish soup, bread, and a spicy pork dish?

_____

_____

_____

2. It's important for some people that they not eat meat. These people— vegetarians—have convictions about not killing and eating animals. One of the major Protestant churches adheres to this dietary restriction. Which one is it?

_____

3. Diabetics also have to be careful of what they eat. Whose responsibility is it—the person doing the inviting or the person being invited—to determine if there will be any problem with the food being served in a home? Explain your reasons.

_____

_____

_____

4. In what ways can we respect cultural differences in others, besides determining whether they can eat certain foods? Give as many ways as you can think of.

_____

_____

_____

Fish for Dinner:
Respect for Cultural Differences

The Story

You yourself may have been in the embarrassing position of either not being able to eat what someone has served or of serving a dish someone can't eat. More and more people are becoming particular about their diet or have restrictions, and such awkward moments are becoming increasingly common.

Our purpose in this story is not to single out any particular religious or ethnic group, but to point out that, because we live in a society with many cultures, we must be aware of differences and be considerate of those people who follow certain customs closely.

The Questions

Orthodox Jews are forbidden to eat shellfish, but they can eat fish with scales and fins. They are able to eat the meat of animals that chew their cuds and have cleft hooves, such as cattle and sheep; but they do not eat pork or pork products. Because fish is a staple food of many Asians, Tom's mother might serve some kind of fish at most dinners.

It wouldn't be too surprising if one or more of your students is following a vegetarian or semi-vegetarian diet. If you do have someone in your class who doesn't eat meat, it would be worthwhile getting the vegetarian viewpoint. The Seventh Day Adventist Church prohibits their members from eating meat.

Probably the most provocative question asked in this unit is the one about who bears the bigger responsibility for communicating dietary restrictions—the person inviting or the person being invited. When it is not obvious to the host, the guest should say that there are certain foods that he or she cannot eat because of health, religion, or conviction. In some social circles the host may routinely inquire of guests about restrictions, but often the host wants to surprise and please guests with special dishes.

You might want to allow your students a good bit of time in which to answer the question about how we can respect cultural differences in others. In the past decade or so, a tremendous amount of thinking and action has been generated on the matter of cultural diversity. It figures, then, that the question can be answered in a cursory fashion or it can become a worthwhile assignment in itself.

An excellent resource about cultural differences is *Respecting Our Differences* by Lynn Duvall (Minneapolis: Free Spirit Publishing, 1994).

References

Day, N. *Violence in Schools*. Springfield, NJ: Enslow Publishers, 1996.

Duvall, L. *Respecting Our Differences*. Minneapolis: Free Spirit Publishing, 1994.

Hirsch, E. D. *Cultural Literacy and the Idea of General Education*. Chicago: University of Chicago Press, 1988.

Hirsch, E. D. *Cultural Literacy: What Every American Needs to Know*. Boston: Houghton Mifflin, 1987.

Rochester, J. M. *Class Warfare*. San Francisco: Encounter Books, 2002.

An Activity about Prejudice

Many years ago a teacher conducted a marvelous, eye-opening experiment with his class. He wanted his students to experience day-by-day prejudice in their own classroom. After a discussion of the pernicious effects of prejudice, the teacher asked his students if they would like to find out how arbitrary and effective prejudicial attitudes are. The blue-eyed students would be the "different" ones, and they would be discriminated against in everything that took place in school—that is, treated in a different way from their classmates. The experiment was all too successful, and the blue-eyed students suffered in ways that they weren't aware of before.

You might also conduct a less involving, but nevertheless enlightening, activity. After a brief discussion of different kinds of prejudice, make a list on the board of all of the prejudices that your students can think of. If gender is listed, then *every* student will see that he or she is subject to one or more kinds of prejudices. The list could look something like this:

gender	race
ethnic background	religion (including atheism and agnosticism)
weight	height
scholastic ability	name
dress (attire)	taste in music
eyeglasses	appliances for teeth
neighborhood	pitch of voice
financial status of family	social status of family
physical attractiveness	athletic ability
pigeon-toed walk	bow-legged walk
hairiness	political views
cleanliness	health
complexion (acne)	accent (regional or national)

Ask if anyone is subject to only one kind of prejudice.

For the Teacher

A rural community in a western U.S. state was the setting for a type of discrimination that is very rare in cities. Because the principal of the public high school was also the religious leader of the community, and because classes in religion were conducted on the school site after school as well as on Thursday afternoons (permitted by state law), those young people who didn't belong to the principal's church felt like outcasts. Their parents complained, and the school district was investigated by the state department of education. The main reason for the investigation was that the young people who didn't go to the classes in religion at the school or attend the principal's church were pressured to do so by the students and by the principal himself, and if they resisted they were vilified by their fellow students. As hard as it is to believe, this took place only a few years ago.

Service, Please

Ashley and Tom decided they needed time to study for a history test, so they went to a small cafe not far away. When they entered the cafe, the owner eyed them in a way that didn't make them feel welcome. There were three or four couples at the tables, but there were plenty of empty tables in the cafe. Three of the tables were near a window overlooking a garden.

"Would you like something?" the owner asked without enthusiasm.

"Yes, we'd like to get a soda and maybe a little something to eat," answered Tom.

"Well. Come this way," said the owner, and led them to a table near the swinging doors that led to the kitchen.

"Can't we sit near the window?" asked Ashley.

"No, those seats are reserved," the owner responded.

Ashley and Tom just looked at each other and sat down at the table next to the kitchen.

Name _____ Date _____

Service, Please: Student Responses

Think about your answers to the following questions and write your response to each.

1. Did Ashley and Tom experience discrimination? Explain.

_____

_____

_____

2. Would you have sat down at the table near the kitchen? Tell why or why not.

_____

_____

_____

3. Why did the owner give Tom and Ashley one of the least desirable tables? Give at least three possible explanations.

_____

_____

_____

4. What is a good way to handle a situation like this?

_____

_____

_____

Service, Please:
Respect for Young People

The Story

Have you ever had a similar experience in a restaurant or cafe? If you can add to the discussion by relating a personal story of discrimination, it will increase your students' involvement in this unit. It happens, even to those people who very rarely experience any kind of overt discrimination.

By the way, is it a matter of discrimination when a man can't enter a swanky restaurant if he isn't wearing a tie?

The Questions

There are many forms of discrimination in our society, some subtle and some blatant. Young people experience age discrimination in various ways, including those that are quite legal, such as being unable to purchase cigarettes when under the age of 18 (or 21) and being unable to attend X-rated and R-rated films. The fact that both Ashley and Tom are members of racial minorities probably didn't influence the cafe owner when he or she gave them an undesirable table, but we can't be sure that that kind of prejudice didn't play a part, consciously or unconsciously, in the owner's behavior.

The second question posed to your students is a difficult one. However, it might be easy for them to say that they would demand a table by the window or else leave. If your students were in the same position, at the age of twelve or thirteen, it could be hard for them to take a stand. At thirteen, not many boys or girls are able to assert themselves in a public place without the support of others. Accompanied by four or five other young people, they might be less acquiescent.

Your students will probably offer prejudice regarding Ashley's and Tom's ages and their racial backgrounds as reasons for the owner's behavior. There is a third reason, of course, and that is that the two young people appeared to be customers who wouldn't spend much money.

An Activity about Considering Others

The handout on pages 34–35 requires your students to put themselves in the places of seven individuals who are in various dilemmas. Each situation, which is only briefly sketched, puts the individual in a position that requires him or her to at least give some thought to the matter of considering others. Considering others is a broad concept, ranging from considering the rights of others to considering their prejudices.

ACTIVITY

_____   _____
                Name   Date

Service, Please: An Activity about Considering Others

Consideration of Others

Considering others is nearly always a good idea—both for the sake of just getting along amicably with people and for being successful in your endeavors. Ignoring the feelings and interests of others indicates that you are self-centered and selfish—and perhaps arrogant as well.

Put yourself in the following situations and decide how much consideration you should accord to others. This consideration includes the feelings, rights, tastes, opinions, and prejudices of other people. Examine each situation thoughtfully and then rate the amount of consideration of others that should be given according to this scale:

1 – Disregard others entirely

2 – Give a little consideration

3 – Give some consideration

4 – Give quite a lot of consideration

5 – Give the utmost consideration

1. You have been the driver of a city bus for ten years. As the years have gone by, you have become very familiar with the riders on your route, many of whom are elderly. Your supervisor has reprimanded you recently for being a little late in running your route.

Rating: _____

_____   _____
Name   Date

2. You are thirteen years old and quite big for your age. Most people assume that you are sixteen or seventeen. All of the other kids in the neighborhood are younger than ten, and they all want to play with you. You very often don't want to be bothered, but all of the parents like you and encourage you to play with their children.

Rating: _____

3. You are in charge of a party for your friends at a popular lake just outside town. The party will take place at the beach and will include about twenty young people. The beach is public and is popular with all ages.

Rating: _____

4. You are at a dinner with your parents, two uncles, and two aunts. The chief topic of conversation all through the meal is about how impolite young people are. You are the only young person at the table.

Rating: _____

5. You are a divorced mother of two small children and need a job desperately. You have a mind of your own and like to dress very casually, but in applying for a job as a dentist's receptionist, you realize that certain things will be expected of you regarding dress, language, and manners.

Rating: _____

6. You are running for office as a city council member. Because there has been a great controversy over the proposed creation by the city of a park in a privileged neighborhood, you are asked to take a stand concerning the issue. Your own inclination is to allow the park into the neighborhood, but the people who are financing your bid for office are mostly opposed to it.

Rating: _____

7. You are an artist and have been generally unsuccessful in selling your work. After a memorable trip to the coast, you decide to paint one of the scenes you recall in your own particular style, which is "abstract" or "non-objective."

Rating: _____

A Sweet Find

Ashley and Becky had come by car with Becky's parents from Canyonville to Grapevine, a town of about 10,000 people 300 miles away. Because it was a hot day in August, they wanted to go to the sweet shop for some ice cream when Becky's mother and father decided to browse in the town's shops. Grapevine was known as a quaint town, with a lovely plaza rimmed by attractive shops.

As the girls finished their ice cream and rose to leave the sweet shop, Ashley spotted something on the seat of the adjacent booth. It was a large brown envelope.

"Look Becky," said Ashley. "That woman who was sitting there a few minutes ago must have left that envelope!"

"Uh-huh. She left about five minutes ago . . . she's probably a long ways from here now," replied Becky.

"We'd better take a look at it. Maybe her name will be on the envelope," suggested Ashley.

Picking up the envelope, Ashley felt a thickness that surprised her. "Wow! I think it's full of money!"

"Here—let's see if there is a name and address," Becky said. "Sure is! The name is Ms. Gloria Anthony, and the address is 420 E. Burnside St., Newbridge. Let's tell the lady at the cash register what we've found."

"Yes, girls," said the shop's owner, "I'll be happy to get in touch with her. I'd never seen her before, I'm afraid."

"Thanks a lot," chirped Becky. "We're just about to leave town with my parents. We just stopped for an hour or so because we heard that Grapevine is a nice place."

"Let me take your names. I'm sure Ms. Anthony would like to know who was so honest in getting this package back to her . . . especially if its money."

Ms. Anthony was *very* happy to get a call from the sweet shop's owner because the envelope contained $2,000 she had meant to deposit in her checking account in Newbridge. It was given to her at the real estate office two doors down from the sweet shop as "earnest money" on a lot she was selling in Grapevine.

Name   **Date**

A Sweet Find: Student Responses

Think about your answers to the following questions and write your response to each.

1. Have you heard or read a story similar to this one? If so, give a brief account of it.

_____

_____

_____

_____

_____

2. How unusual were Becky and Ashley in trying to return the money to Ms. Anthony? Would most young people do the same? Why do you think so?

_____

_____

_____

3. Would you have returned the money?

_____

_____

4. Is this story about respect in any way? In what way?

_____

_____

_____

A Sweet Find:
Respect for the Property of Others

The Story

The most transportable form of property is money, and one of its distinguishing features is that possessing it is usually a temporary matter. Our five-dollar bill, in spite of serial numbers, looks just like yours. In contrast, our ring, car, or sweater can probably be distinguished from yours by a cursory inspection. So when you find three bills on the street, it's very difficult to know how to return the money to the unlucky owner, especially because ownership of those bills is so fleeting and anonymous. Thus Becky and Ashley could have been tempted to split the money, which was not their property, and have been wealthier for the find.

As you know, accounts of honesty such as this one are regularly published in newspapers. This story was printed in Grapevine's little newspaper as a result of Ms. Anthony's letting the sweet shop owner know of her gratitude and because she wanted the public to know of the girls' honesty. Yes, there was a reward.

The Questions

As noted above, stories of both young and older people going out of their way to be honest and return money to rightful owners is almost commonplace. But it still is unusual enough to be considered newsworthy. Your students probably can cite an instance similar to the one in this story.

Becky and Ashley might have been somewhat remarkable because they weren't residents of the town in which they found the money. They would have been out of town in 15 minutes, with the money, if they had been different people. A certain sense of pride in her or his hometown can nudge a person into returning money in a situation such as this one. We won't guess whether your students will believe that most young people would have returned the $2,000. Actually, none of us really knows what we'll do until we're in that situation.

Maybe the third question could be the subject of a short writing exercise, to be written by and for the student only. It wouldn't need to be shared with you or the class—it's just an exercise in examining a situation in which conflicting emotions erupt in the individual.

The story is supposed to be about respecting an individual's right to retain his or her property. It's also about honesty, of course. Perhaps the ethical question of whether it is wrong to keep the money can be debated, but the argument for keeping the money, on purely ethical grounds, is weak. When owners are careless about their property, does this absolve from blame someone who takes advantage of that carelessness? There are countless examples of that situation at school, such as when students leave clothing, equipment, and personal articles behind or unattended. Is it our fault when we don't lock our car's doors and our car is stolen? What do you think?

For the Teacher

An Activity about Honesty

First, distribute the handout on pages 41–42 to your class. After students respond to it on their own, begin a whole-class discussion. Some classes will be taken in by the changing persona of the individual losing the ten-dollar bill. Other classes with a little training in logic or ethics will be more sophisticated. As the students continue to discuss the questions, guide them to see that from a moral point of view, it doesn't matter who drops the bill.

ACTIVITY

Name

Date

A Sweet Find: An Activity about Honesty

What Would You Do If You Found Money That Wasn't Yours?

Noah was walking along a bumpy sidewalk one day, about thirty feet behind a stranger, a boy about his age, when he noticed something flutter behind the boy. As he approached the spot where the thing fell, Noah became more and more convinced it was money. Sure enough, when he reached down, it turned out to be a ten-dollar bill. Noah hesitated a second. Should he run up to the boy and tell him he dropped some money?

1. What would you do?

_____

_____

2. What would you do if, instead of a boy, it was a well-dressed older man who dropped the money?

_____

_____

ACTIVITY

From *Respect Matters*, Copyright © Good Year Books. This page may be reproduced for classroom use only by the actual purchaser of the book. www.goodyearbooks.com.

_____   _____
            Name   **Date**

3. What would you do if it were a girl, about three years older than you are, who dropped the ten-dollar bill?

_____

_____

4. What if it were someone you knew—a mentally challenged boy a little older than you are?

_____

_____

5. What if, instead of a stranger, it were a good friend?

_____

_____

_____

6. What if a known gang member with a very bad reputation dropped the bill?

_____

_____

7. What if it were a friend's brother that you were following?

_____

_____

8. What if it were someone you disliked very much?

_____

_____

No T-shirts

Ashley, treasurer of the dance club, phoned the Everything in T-Shirts Company about ordering t-shirts for all ten members of the club. She reached the firm on a Friday afternoon.

"Hello. Is this the Everything in T-Shirts Company?" she asked.

"Yes," answered the woman in an indifferent voice.

"I understand from your ad that if I order ten medium t-shirts of our own design that we can get a 20% reduction in price. Is that right?"

"No, we can't do that now," returned the woman.

"But that's what your ad said, and I've just collected the money from the members of my club," protested Ashley.

"Sorry," the woman said sourly. "We can't honor that ad. I have a call on another line now. I have to go. Goodbye."

On the next day, Ashley went down to the store and asked for the manager. He explained that the store was going out of business and that they only had six medium t-shirts left.

_____ _____
Name   **Date**

No T-shirts: **Student Responses**

Think about your answers to the following questions and write your response to each.

1. Why didn't the woman answering the phone at the Everything in T-Shirts Company explain why she couldn't fill the order?

_____

_____

2. Do you think her attitude was affected by the fact that the store was going out of business? Explain.

_____

_____

_____

3. Do you think the fact that Ashley sounded young on the phone had anything to do with the manner of the woman answering the phone?

_____

_____

4. What do you think the manager did to satisfy Ashley?

_____

_____

5. What would you do if you were Ashley?

_____

_____

No T-shirts:
Courtesy

The Story

Perhaps it's because of all the advertising the telephone companies do, but we notice that phoning is more prominent in our culture than at any other time. You can see people with cellular phones in cars, on trains, in malls, on the streets, on airplanes, and in the parks. It's as if they are afraid to go out without their phones, and that is probably true.

What the ads don't mention is that communicating by telephone requires a particular etiquette, just as face-to-face conversation does. There is a proper way to speak on the telephone, both for the caller and the person receiving the call. The proliferation of phones seems to have been accompanied by a slow disappearance of the skills of politely communicating on the telephone.

This story is about one little part of the large problem of businesses communicating with customers. Some are would-be customers, as in the case of a firm's soliciting business on the phone ("telemarketing") either with live personnel or automated recordings. Most people find telemarketing to be a big headache and an invasion of their privacy. But Ashley had the old kind of problem—someone just didn't bother to be polite to her on the phone.

The Questions

The woman who took Ashley's call may have been harried or distracted. She may also have been embarrassed to tell Ashley why she couldn't fill the order. The woman might well have been in a bad mood because she was about to lose her job.

Often we have to make an effort to be polite when we don't feel like it. If you've ever encountered a clerk on an "off" day, you know that the clerk who doesn't make an effort can easily let his or her mood show through. You have probably been on both sides of this kind of interaction and recall very well when, as a clerk, your attitude upset customers.

Often people talking on the telephone with people they don't know will make assumptions. A young voice may give them a certain impression. If the older person has a prejudice against young people, that attitude can influence the way she or he behaves.

The manager was not able to give Ashley ten t-shirts. Whether or not he tried to mollify her by offering an alternative is conjectural. If he's as accommodating as many business people are, he might have suggested another store or even phone another store to see if it can handle Ashley's order.

The last question is as open-ended as any in this book. We hope your students will suggest that Ashley can gracefully thank the manager and try to get the t-shirts elsewhere.

For the Teacher

An Activity about Telephoning

The logical way to follow up this unit is with a lesson about telephone courtesy. Such a lesson was once common in the middle grades, and sometimes high school teachers attempted to go over the basics of telephone courtesy with their classes. The lesson is probably most effective when it incorporates role-playing with real or imaginary telephones. Your students may hesitate to role-play, but it certainly wouldn't be anything unusual for them to carry on a phone conversation, even if it isn't the real thing.

Stress the importance of the opening of any phone conversation. It is polite to let the person receiving the call know immediately from whom the call is coming. ("Identify yourself first.") Go over all of the usual points about speaking distinctly, not keeping people waiting, listening carefully and not interrupting, keeping the length of the conversation limited so other people can use the line, having a pad and pencil ready so you can take notes, and giving the other person a chance to contribute to the conversation (some people, with a telephone in their hands, hold monologues). Because we rely on the telephone so much, it is incumbent that adults instruct young people about proper phone use.

Even though this lesson has not discussed whether courtesy is simply an outward manifestation of respect, you can ask your students to distinguish between the two concepts. In some ways, they are synonymous, even though respect is much deeper and broader.

Sweets

On their way home from school, Becky and Tanya decided to buy some candy at the neighborhood drug store. As they entered the store, they caught a glimpse of the pained expression on the face of Mr. Knowles, the manager, and simultaneously they heard a loud wail to their right. A young girl, about five years old, was crying loudly while her red-faced mother stood a few feet away, looking distraught.

"You *said* I could have a peanut butter 'n' choc'lit cup. Now you won't buy it for me!" the child blubbered.

"But, darling, you heard the man—they are out of that kind of candy. Why don't you pick out a candy bar? See—those are all your favorites there," the mother said, pointing to the large selection of candy bars.

"I don't *want* a candy bar! I want a peanut butter-choc'lit cup!" shouted the girl.

"Please listen, honey. There aren't any peanut butter-chocolate cups in the store. Isn't there anything else you'd like to have?" her mother pleaded.

"No! No! No!! You never give me anything I want—never! I wish you weren't my mother!" sobbed the child.

Tanya and Becky looked at each other, then turned around and walked out of the store. Both of them had younger brothers and sisters, and they didn't want to witness another temper tantrum.

Name

Date

Sweets: Student Responses

Think about your answers to the following questions and write your response to each.

1. Have you witnessed a scene similar to the one Tanya and Becky saw in the drug store? If so, when did it happen and what was the cause of the child's unhappiness?

_____

_____

_____

_____

2. Is the little girl aware that she is embarrassing her mother? What makes you think so?

_____

_____

_____

3. If the child makes a habit of throwing temper tantrums in public places, what can her mother do to curb or stop this behavior? What, if anything, can Mr. Knowles, the store manager, do about the situation?

_____

_____

_____

_____

Sweets:
Respect for Parents

The Story

Some people think that people older than fifty believe that the majority of young people in our country are either neglected by their parents or that parents are being bullied by their children (and sometimes both). We see kids terrorizing their parents far too often. Of course, the five-year-old in the story represents the kind of child who has plagued parents for as long as our society has existed. Once a child realizes she or he has the upper hand, parents are going to be miserable.

If a child is brought up to respect her or his parents, that child will be unlikely to humiliate the parents in public. There will be a feeling of being proud to be the offspring of the parent. But it is so much easier to say children should be respectful of their parents than it is to ensure that the respect is implanted and grows. Fortunately, in the child's late teens and early twenties, the respect often does grow.

The Questions

It is very likely that your students can relate a good many stories similar to this one about the little girl making a big fuss in the store. Perhaps your only problem will be in limiting the amount of time spent recalling scenes of spoiled children.

The little girl is very much aware that she has put her mother in an embarrassing and powerless position. Your students will grasp the idea that children deliberately create scenes in public places for a variety of reasons, some of which have to do with power. Maybe some of them have done it themselves. In fact, if they are honest, several will admit it.

Perhaps the most interesting question is the one asking what the mother can do to curb or stop this bratty behavior from recurring. Students' suggestions should be terribly illuminating, whether they are wise or misguided in their responses.

An Activity about Respecting Parents

Distribute the handout on pages 51–52 to students and ask them to read the scenarios. Then lead a whole-class discussion about each example.

This activity could spark some animated discussion among your students because most of the young people who are described aren't really exhibiting much respect for their parents. Accordingly, there should be some head-scratching as to whether borrowing a tie or complimenting a mother about her spaghetti constitutes genuine respect. Does Loretta show respect for her father when she borrows money from her mother in order to get him a "good" birthday present?

Out of the discussion, however, your students should reveal what they think constitutes respecting one's parents. There may be little consensus about the matter, but the discussion should open students' eyes to how they can be respectful of their own parents.

Name   Date

Sweets: An Activity about Respecting Parents

Respecting Parents

1. Which of these young people are showing genuine respect for a parent? Explain your answer.

- Melanie asks her mother to help her decide which clothes to wear when she spends the weekend with Jocelyn.

- Julius writes about his father when Ms. Glover assigns the topic, "The Person I Admire Most," for a writing assignment.

- Nicholas asks his father if he may borrow a red tie for a special date.

- Sam tells his mother that he likes the way she cooks spaghetti.

- Loretta borrows ten dollars from her mother to add to her own five dollars so she can give her father a good birthday present.

_____

_____

_____

_____

_____

ACTIVITY

| Name | Date |

2. Which son or daughter has shown the most respect? Why do you think so?

_____

_____

_____

_____

_____

_____

_____

_____

Billy the Bully

S orry, I don't get it, Ms. Gomez," Victor said in a subdued voice.

"You *never* get it, Victor," taunted a sturdy, red-headed boy two seats back. "When was the last time you knew the answer?"

"That's enough, Billy," the teacher said firmly. "We can work on the problem a little later, Victor."

It often happened like that. Victor, a nice-looking blond boy, was not able to respond aloud correctly or to do a simple assignment, in spite of working hard at home with his mother to learn math, spelling, and history. Both Ms. Gomez and Victor's mother were certain that he could learn the basic facts if he'd work even harder.

School might have been bearable for Victor if it weren't for Billy—like the time he took his turn at the chalkboard in a word game that Ms. Gomez was fond of having her students play. In the game students compose a story by consecutively adding to a few words that have been written on the chalkboard. For example, Ms. Gomez might write "Suddenly she heard . . ." and a student would come up to the board and add "a strange noise in the house. . . ." Another student would add a few more words (with punctuation, if needed), and so on until the story reached a satisfactory conclusion.

On this particular day, Victor had responded to the question for his side with "ther aren't no lakes ther." Billy, who was bright and aggressive at school but browbeaten by his older brother at home, had laughed hard with the others and then said, "Don't you know how to spell there, Victor? Oh, that's right—you can barely read."

Actually, he was reading almost at grade level, but his spelling was very poor. Victor's face turned red, and he clenched his fists. Billy knew that Victor wouldn't retaliate, however. Victor was at least 15 pounds lighter than Billy, and he was the kind of boy who took insults without fighting back with either his fists or words.

Going to school was very painful for Victor. He did have some friends, but they just accepted him as being "slow" and didn't try to stick up for him. None of his friends was brave enough to tell Billy to stop riding him. Victor had some good qualities. He was quite amiable when he wasn't teased, and he knew a lot about cars. Moreover, Victor was not a bad athlete for a boy his size; he was a consistent hitter and fielder in softball. Unfortunately for him, there was a lot more than softball going on at school.

_____   _____
Name   **Date**

Billy the Bully: Student Responses

Think about your answers to the following questions and write your response to each.

1. What can anyone do to help Victor?

_____

_____

_____

2. Once Billy looked at Victor and sneered, "Why do they call you Victor? When was the last time you beat anybody?" What would you say if you were Victor?

_____

_____

_____

_____

3. It is said that a bully is covering up feelings of inferiority. He or she picks on people that he or she has good reason to believe won't stand up for themselves. We think most often about bullies who physically intimidate, and sometimes hurt, others; but there are other kinds of bullies. Name two or three.

_____

_____

_____

_____

For the Teacher

Billy the Bully:
Respect for an Individual's Worth

The Story

Your first reaction to the story might be that the teacher isn't doing much to stop Billy's hazing of Victor. That might also be the reaction of some of your students, although they will probably be thinking in terms of how some youngsters seem to naturally pick on others and how some kids seem always to be targets for put-downs and ridicule. That kind of behavior is hardly new, but it seems that more and more new books and media reports are devoted to this subject than ever before.

The Questions

Nasty remarks have no place in a civil classroom, and it would seem that Ms. Gomez should not allow Billy's jibes and insults. Nevertheless, a teacher can only do so much in setting a positive tone in class. A teacher cannot control what happens before and after school and at recess. A teacher can set an example, and she or he can communicate clearly that only positive remarks are acceptable.

Taunts such as Billy's about Victor's name are commonplace in most schools. For various psychological reasons, young people such as Billy seem to need someone to pick on, often for the sake of their egos. This behavior can be seen most often in the downtrodden looking for even less fortunate individuals whom they can "lord it over."

We hope your students recognize that there are other bullies in addition to the physical kind, namely those who bully by virtue of their intellectual superiority, their higher occupational rank, their higher social positions, or by having someone depend on them financially or emotionally. It is doubtful if they will use those particular words, but your students probably can paint good word pictures of these non-physical bullies. Whenever one individual is decidedly stronger than another in a social, physical, intellectual, emotional, financial, or psychological way, there is an opportunity for bullying.

A Writing Activity about Freedom from Harassment

You might tie in this story with a stimulating language arts activity dealing with fables. After your students have reacted to the questions about the story, invite them to write a fable with a moral such as: "The most powerful person is not always the happiest." To refresh their memories about fables, read one of Aesop's fables. Remind them that a fable teaches a lesson and its characters are usually animals who talk and act like human beings.

For those who are not "self-starters," the characters in the story can be used as prototypes for the animal characters in the fable they make up. There are a few bullies in the animal kingdom, for example, and so the character of Billy might be portrayed by a frigate bird, a pit bull, a killer whale (orca), or a wolverine. Others who need help getting started can use a suitable Aesop fable and modify it so that the characters represent respect, esteem, caution, or intimidation. Students can illustrate their fables; some may be more enthusiastic about drawing the animal characters than about writing the fables themselves.

References

De Roin, N. *Jataka Tales*. Boston: Houghton-Mifflin, 1975.

Kent, J. (Illus.). *Fables of Aesop*. New York: Pantheon, 1973.

Leaf, M. *Aesop's Fables*. New York: The Heritage Reprints, 1941.

Reeves, J. *Fables from Aesop*. New York: Walch, 1962.

Untermeyer, L. *Aesop's Fables*. New York: Golden Press, 1966.

Saplings and Cans

Becky and Ashley decided to spend a day hiking along the river. Although Becky had done a good deal of hiking and camping, Ashley's family rarely left the city limits of their town, and she knew little about the out-of-doors. Becky had loaned Ashley a backpack, which contained food and a few tools.

When they had started down the path from the road, heading toward the river, the girls encountered a sapling that was leaning over and blocking their way. They stopped and looked at the young alder tree.

"Here, I'll chop its trunk so we can pull it away and get by," Ashley offered.

"No, Ashley. It's just fallen over because of that downpour we had last week. The ground got very wet and the soil washed away from the roots. I'll prop it up, and it will be all right," Becky answered.

She then pushed up the little tree, making it upright, and took a small shovel from her pack. Then she brought some earth to the base of the tree and tamped the loose earth until it was firm around the base of the sapling.

"That should give it a chance," Becky said.

When they reached the river, their path met another little path that followed the river. After hiking about a hundred yards, Becky suddenly stopped. She picked up a can and a small object near it.

"I hate these things!" Becky exclaimed, picking up a pull ring from a pop can and putting it and the can in her backpack. "Little fish push their heads through the hole, and then they can't get the ring off. Then, as they grow, the ring strangles them to death!"

RESPONSES

_____   _____
Name   **Date**

Saplings and Cans: Student Responses

Think about your answers to the following questions and write your
response to each.

1. Do you think Becky was being silly about the little tree? Will it really
be all right? Explain why you think so.

_____

_____

_____

_____

2. What other refuse causes death to living creatures in the water?

_____

_____

_____

3. What can be done about all of the cans and pull rings that end up in
streams, rivers, lakes, and oceans?

_____

_____

_____

_____

Saplings and Cans:
Respect for Living Things

The Story

"Becky" exhibits some of the characteristics found in Howard Gardner's eighth intelligence, "the naturalist." The outing that she and Ashley embark upon starts with an encounter with a leaning sapling and is soon followed by another with a discarded can. It is just about impossible to find any place, even in the areas set aside as wilderness, where the ground isn't littered or the flora scarred. Accordingly, this story can strike some of your students as so commonplace as to be very uninteresting. There might be some students, however, who feel strongly about protecting our natural heritage. Every generation apparently must learn, as the ones before it, that our natural resources can't be taken for granted. According to The Audubon Society, the Nature Conservancy, The Wilderness Society, and other groups, we must remain constantly vigilant in protecting our forests, streams, lakes, rivers, and wildlife.

The Questions

The first question about whether Becky was being silly in propping up the little tree will be taken seriously by those students who love trees and the out-of-doors. We ask it only because people do hack away at small trees and underbrush that is in their way. Some trees are removed purposely to admit light into areas with too much growth, but for some of us it is painful to find saplings cut down needlessly.

Your students should have little trouble in naming the connected plastic rings that hold the necks of cans in six-packs as being another killer of fish, birds, and other creatures that live in or near the water. Their other responses could include nets and antifreeze containers (the remaining contents of which seep into streams and lakes).

The answer to the third question will be hard to come up with because the problem is as bad as it ever was. Perhaps your students can contribute a solution that the manufacturers and environmentalists will welcome.

A Nature Walk Activity

A logical activity that can confirm or refute the experience of Becky and Ashley in the story is for your students to spent a certain amount of time—five minutes, ten minutes, a half hour—walking along any path outside the city limits of your community. They can note—and remove—any debris they find during that period of time. It would be best if they do not go on highways or on roads. Litter patrols on freeways, for instance, might have recently swept up the refuse, and, of course, they would not be safe on a busy highway.

Unless your class is enthusiastic about "cleaning up the environment," a five-minute or a ten-minute weekend survey, with the litter returned to the classroom, would be sufficient to corroborate the experience of the girls in the story. Suggest that your students go out in pairs with adult supervision, and so that the teams don't duplicate their itineraries, assign different areas outside the city to the various teams.

Students can tabulate results and place pins on a map showing where they found the refuse. A follow-up story in the school newspaper could be reported by a student who writes well and is enthusiastic about the findings.

Ripped!

Marvin didn't always come to school in fashionable clothes and his clothes were a little too well pressed, but he was polite to the teachers and he tried to get along with the other students. Unfortunately, being polite to teachers didn't endear Marvin to his classmates. Most of them hadn't cared for their teachers since the second grade. And his classmates weren't too kind to Marvin when he tried to talk to them—the girls as well as the boys. He was different.

Marvin hummed Mozart arias at his desk and in the hallways. He didn't try to play baseball or football at recess, preferring to stand near the playground equipment or to talk with the adult supervising the yard. When he got the right answers in class, the other students tried to make fun of him, calling him a "nerd" and worse. During physical education classes, he was jeered at and taunted when he didn't get a hit or catch a ball. He knew more about computers than anyone in the school, including the teachers, but his classmates didn't let him tell them anything about how to run the programs for the classroom computer.

Even though his teachers and his parents knew he was being ostracized, they didn't know how to make the situation better. A crisis developed one day in the crowded hallway when someone managed to rip Marvin's jacket pocket without his seeing who did it—not that Marvin would have dared to report the student anyway.

_____   Name   Date   _____

Ripped!: Student Responses

Think about your answers to the following questions and write your response to each.

1. Is there anything Marvin can do to become better liked and less of an outcast?

_____

_____

_____

2. Is ridicule the worse form of disrespect? Explain.

_____

_____

_____

3. There probably are some things that the teachers can do to help Marvin become more accepted. What are they?

_____

_____

_____

4. Is the best solution for Marvin to go to another school or to be homeschooled? Why do you think so?

_____

_____

_____

Ripped!:
Respect for the Feelings of Others

The Story

All of the details about the persecution of Marvin are true, but that may not surprise you. We all know kids can be cruel. We don't think it is appropriate for youngsters to taunt, torment, and ridicule other young people. We think they should be inherently kind, even though we know that what's taught at home and their experiences in the world can influence them to behave in cruel ways. We know that their parents, for instance, can inculcate hatred in them for another group of people. This is based on a real incident, and in that boy's case, racial animosity was a factor. That isn't mentioned in the story, but a juvenile group very often persecutes its own members, and sometimes the reasons aren't clear to adults.

The Questions

Perhaps the situation in which Marvin found himself is the most difficult for a young student. There have been reports of teachers persecuting students, but that isn't as shattering as being ridiculed by your peers. Your students may have some good suggestions about how Marvin can get along with his classmates. (The adults in the real Marvin's school couldn't come up with anything that helped.)

Ridicule is hard to eradicate in society because it satisfies the base need of some persons to try to be superior to those who are easy targets by virtue of their appearance, manners, circumstances, or even talents. However, you can hope to give your students a keener awareness of the harm that ridicule does by reflecting about the presence of ridicule in the school and in the community. Has it touched anyone in your class? Will they speak out about it?

Many people believe that ridicule is the worst form of disrespect. It hurts most of all. Your students will probably agree, and you'll be interested in the reasons they give.

Logically, there are strategies that Marvin's teachers can use to alleviate the pain of a student's being ostracized and ridiculed. The experts in these matters might offer theoretical suggestions about giving Marvin a chance to associate with one or two of his classmates in situations in which he can be helped or in which he can help them without "lording it over" them. (Actually, Marvin was a naturally modest young man.) As a matter of fact, young people themselves may be more expert in offering advice in a situation as difficult as this. They are more likely to have some insights about what might help Marvin.

After the incident when Marvin's jacket was ripped—and he also received a scratch on his body—he was removed from the school. We don't really want you or your students to be influenced by this fact, however, because every problem such as Marvin's can't be solved by homeschooling or transferring to another school. Somehow we have to do a better job of eliminating these bad situations in our schools.

Leading a Discussion about Kindness

The following questions could be used to start a follow-up discussion after you complete this unit about respect for the feelings of others.

1. When have you been most grateful for an act of kindness?

2. Are there times when you don't want anyone to be kind to you? When do they occur?

3. Do some people know how to be kind better than others? Why is that so?

4. What act of kindness on your part made you happiest?

5. What act of kindness is likely to be futile?

6. Is an act really kindness when the person bestowing it is expecting something in return?

Should Old Acquaintance Be Forgotten?

When Gordon entered a college some 500 miles north of his hometown, he never expected to see someone he knew, and least of all for that person to be on the faculty. But, sure enough, Gordon glimpsed Mr. Halliburton in the bookstore on the first day he attended classes. A slim forty-year-old, Mr. Halliburton had been one of Gordon's middle school teachers and now, six years later, they were teacher and student again—only Gordon wasn't taking any of Mr. Halliburton's classes.

For about a week Gordon worried a little about whether he should look up Mr. Halliburton in his office. He wasn't sure Mr. Halliburton would remember him, and he was a little shy about renewing the acquaintance. As teacher and student, they hadn't been especially close. Gordon was just a fair student in Mr. Halliburton's homeroom class in the seventh grade. Nevertheless, out of boredom and a little curiosity, Gordon overcame his reticence and knocked on Mr. Halliburton's door.

"Come in," welcomed Mr. Halliburton.

Gordon hesitated and then opened the door cautiously. "Hi, Mr. Halliburton. Do you remember me? I was in your homeroom class at North Middle School."

"Uh? Oh, yes. Can't remember your name, though. What is it?"

"Gordon Williams."

"Oh."

Gordon stood awkwardly just inside the door.

"I'm afraid I'm terribly busy right now, Gordon. Nice to see you."

Gordon still stood at the doorway. There was a silence of about twenty awful seconds. Mr. Halliburton started writing on one of the many papers scattered on his desk.

"G-g-goodbye, Mr. Halliburton," Gordon mumbled, turning to go.

There was no reply from the older man. Gordon closed the door quietly and ambled down the corridor. His shoulders were slumped, and there was a frown on his face.

From *Respect Matters*, Copyright © Good Year Books. This page may be reproduced for classroom use only by the actual purchaser of the book. www.goodyearbooks.com.

Name   Date

Should Old Acquaintance Be Forgotten?:
Student Responses

Think about your answers to the following questions and write your response to each.

1. Why didn't Mr. Halliburton offer Gordon a seat and exchange a few remembrances with him?

_____

_____

_____

2. Do you think Gordon should have bothered Mr. Halliburton without asking first for an appointment? Why or why not?

_____

_____

_____

3. Do you consider Mr. Halliburton's behavior rude? What do you think Gordon thought of the experience?

_____

_____

_____

4. What would you do now if you were Gordon?

_____

_____

_____

Should Old Acquaintance Be Forgotten?:
Civility

The Story

To some of your students, this may seem to be a farfetched story, but it isn't. People, including professors, are not always polite. Rudeness is everywhere, but it is particularly hurtful to the young, who may not be used to it.

If we look for them, we can find—or imagine we have encountered—quite a few slights. There are occasions when we can't mistake a discourtesy, of course. That is the point of "Should Old Acquaintance Be Forgotten?" Mr. Halliburton simply didn't bother to spend a few minutes conversing with his former student because he was (a) preoccupied, (b) not a polite person ordinarily, or (c) didn't think enough of Gordon to bother being polite. All Gordon can make of the very brief interview is that he was unworthy of a few moments of Mr. Halliburton's time.

The Questions

In considering the first question, your students may have a hard time accepting Mr. Halliburton's rudeness in dismissing Gordon so peremptorily. They may have heard the admonition, "There's never an excuse for being rude." And, indeed, there is no excuse for Mr. Halliburton's rudeness.

There is an etiquette in most colleges and universities regarding the office hours of faculty members. Gordon may not have know that some faculty members do not like to be interrupted and restrict their interviews with students to the posted office hours.

Most students in your class will be able to identify with Gordon. They've been embarrassed by adults (and probably teachers) in their young lives. Their reactions to this story should be revealing.

The most important question is the last: "What would you do now if you were Gordon?" You might guess how the majority of your students will respond to this question. It also leads in nicely to the following role-playing exercise.

A Role-playing Activity

Role-playing is a most appropriate activity to accompany this unit. Ask for volunteers for the two roles or select two students who would probably profit from role-playing. Because there are only two people in the story, you might involve an additional student by using the Double Technique. One of the actors in the situation is supplied with a double who stands beside the actor and interacts with the actor as himself or herself. The double tries to develop an identity with the actor, speaking the actor's mind and thoughts. In the case of this story, either Gordon or Mr. Halliburton could be assigned a double. By bringing out the actor's "other self," the double helps the actor achieve a new and higher level of understanding.

Generous and Poor

When the students shuffled into the classroom and headed for their desks, one or two glanced up at the chalkboard and saw:

POVERTY PRODUCES FOOLISH GENEROSITY

Becky was one of those who noticed the single sentence on the board. She said to Ashley, "I wonder what that's supposed to mean." At about that time the teacher, Ms. Winters, walked briskly into the classroom and then waited for everyone to take a seat.

"Did any of you notice this sentence behind me?" she asked.

"Oh," grunted Marcus. "No."

The others didn't say anything.

"I'd like you to consider that statement rather carefully," Ms. Winters said quietly.

There was a buzz in the room, and then a pause. Two or three students muttered to each other.

Finally, William, a newcomer to the class since Christmas vacation, growled: "What's that supposed to mean?"

"I wanted you young people to figure it out. What do *you* think, William?" responded Ms. Winters.

"I think it's crazy! Why should poor people be especially generous? Who said that, anyway?" retorted William.

"Well, to tell the truth, I did. At least I thought there might be a relationship between being overly generous and being poor, and I wanted you students to consider it."

"What do you know about being poor, Winters?" demanded William. "I'll bet you've never gone hungry in your life, much less worn old, torn clothes and froze in your house. You don't know what you're talking about, Winters!" blurted out William.

RESPONSES

Name _____   Date _____

Generous and Poor: Student Responses

Think about your answers to the following questions and write your response to each.

1. Is it possible that Ms. Winters does know something about poverty? What about William?

_____

_____

_____

_____

2. How would you describe William's attitude toward Ms. Winters?

_____

_____

_____

3. Is rudeness always a sign of disrespect? Why or why not?

_____

_____

_____

4. Is courtesy *always* a sign of respect? Explain.

_____

_____

_____

Generous and Poor:
Respect for Authority

The Story

The point of the story isn't whether or not poverty promotes foolish generosity. It's about William's lack of respect for Ms. Winters. Ordinarily, students address their teachers as "Mister," Miss," "Missus," or "Mizz." William pointedly only called the teacher by her surname. But his manner was disrespectful, and he seemed to be challenging her authority. If his attitude spreads to other students, Ms. Winters is in for a tough year.

The Questions

The first question is designed to make your students take seriously the idea of a possible relationship between foolish generosity and poverty. It is probably an idea that has never occurred to them. You, however, should take Ms. Winters's position and keep an open mind about the proposition.

In asking whether either Ms. Winters or William has had any firsthand experience with poverty, we invite your students to speculate about why each of them behaves as they do in this little story. Because of his vehemence, it is logical to infer that William has had some experience with poverty, but it is more fascinating to speculate about Ms. Winters.

William's attitude toward Ms. Winters can be described as rude, hostile, disrespectful, and antagonistic. On the other hand, a sympathetic view of William would describe his behavior as being honest, forthright, and heartfelt. In any case, he chose a confrontational way of expressing his view.

One of your students may be able to provide an instance when rudeness is not a manifestation of disrespect. We can't think of any. On the other hand, your students should be able to provide many examples of instances when courtesy doesn't necessarily reflect respect.

An Exercise about Respecting Authority

If there is time, you can administer the exercise on pages 76–77 soon after concluding the discussion about the story. It isn't subtle; it just presents a number of situations in which young people have to accede to authority. The thinking comes when your students decide *why* they obey the authority figure, rule, or law.

ACTIVITY

Name   Date

Generous and Poor: An Activity about Respecting Authority

Just Do as I Say

Everyone, including the president of the United States, is told what to do every day. Most of us don't care to be ordered around, but there seems to be no escaping it. We may not always want to obey someone who is in a position of authority, but we usually do so because that person has some kind of power over us or else we respect the person's right to tell us what to do.

In each of the situations described below, tell if you think the person obeying someone in authority is doing so because of

- respect for the person's position,

- respect for the person as a person,

- respect for the person's knowledge or wisdom, or because of the power the person has.

1. Eating a vegetable because your mother or father tells you it is good for you

_____

2. Brushing your teeth the way your dentist told you to do

_____

Name   Date

3. Refraining from walking across a newly planted lawn in a park when a sign tells you not to

_____

4. Washing up before dinner when told to do so by your mother

_____

5. Wearing shoes in a store because the sign on the door says, "No shoes, no service."

_____

6. Coming out of a game when your coach substitutes another player for you

_____

7. Turning in an assignment on time

_____

8. Pulling a car over to the side of the road when a traffic officer follows in a police car with lights flashing

_____

9. Refraining from running around a swimming pool when the posted rules say you shouldn't

_____

10. Hunting deer or elk only in season and then only with a license

_____

11. Dressing the way you are told to dress for a party by a host or hostess on an invitation

_____

12. Going into a battle at the command of an officer

_____

Nick

Nick was the tallest boy in his class and he was nice looking, but his build was fragile and his complexion was quite pale. His behavior in the classroom and on the playground showed a lack of confidence. Nick's responses to difficult situations were almost always immature. He was tolerated by the girls and shunned by the boys. Nick did associate with two girls who lived in the foster home where Nick had been for a year.

Because Nick was in a class of students who wanted to learn and who were good at learning, he was left on the sidelines. He didn't compete—or even try to compete— with this classmates, accepting the role of an onlooker or outsider. Because there were almost no times during the school day in which he could excel, his attitude was mostly one of sadly accepting his lot—but at times he whined to the teacher and his classmates. Generally speaking, his teacher didn't give a great deal of attention to his complaints.

One afternoon Dennis told Nick that he wasn't needed to play a baseball game the boys were starting, and Nick sobbed. Trish, a very bright and well-adjusted girl, said a few kind words to him on that occasion. His teacher felt sorry for Nick but didn't know what to do to help him.

Name   **Date**

Nick: Student Responses

Think about your answers to the following questions and write your response to each.

1. What are the main reasons for Nick's lack of confidence?

_____

_____

_____

2. Can anything be done to bolster his feeling of self-worth? What do you suggest?

_____

_____

_____

_____

3. What could his teacher have done to help Nick when Dennis refused to let him in the game?

_____

_____

_____

4. Would Nick be better off in another class, where he could possibly gain some status as a student and as a worthwhile human being? Explain.

_____

_____

_____

_____

Nick:
Respect for Self

The Story

Nick's life wasn't a happy one. Can anyone truly be happy without self-respect?

Nick exemplifies the loner and misfit. The tragedy was that forces beyond his control created a young man who was ill-equipped to cope with the ordinary problems of growing up in our society. The real Nick was a discarded child—an orphan who was placed in a home for the children of unwed Asian mothers and American servicemen—the deck was stacked against him.

The Questions

Your students can infer a number of factors that had completely eroded any self-confidence Nick may have had as a young child. He didn't live with his parents but with other children who had been separated from their parents. Nick wasn't athletic; and his schoolwork was poor, whereas most of his classmates did work that was well above average. (Trish, the girl who was kind to him, obtained a perfect score on the California Test of Mental Maturity that year.) To top it off, Nick was apparently friendless.

Although there is no shortage these days of programs for enhancing the self-esteem of young people in the schools, most of them may be missing the point. You feel like a worthwhile person when you are able to do worthwhile things. Artificial honors, awards, and programs with posters and slogans are only temporary measures to boost sagging egos. If there is an atmosphere of support and security, the enhancing of self-esteem is more likely to be lasting. What *can* be done is for young people to become more supportive of one another. That can be a matter of only one or two youngsters being aware of the emotional needs of their classmates.

Nick was in a high-achieving class where academic excellence was about as important as athletic prowess. Having neither an exceptionally quick mind nor an athletic body, Nick was bound to suffer in comparison with his classmates. It is possible that he would have benefitted from a move to another class. He was placed in the class he was in, however, because the principal thought that his teacher would be able to work well with Nick. As it turned out, the teacher was only moderately successful in helping Nick adjust academically and socially.

Neill and Stor offer practical techniques for enhancing self-esteem. In contrast, Rochester debunks the whole idea.

References

Neill, K., & Stor, S. "Teaching Techniques." *Journal of School Health* 73 (December 2003): 392.

Rochester, J. M. *Class Warfare*. San Francisco: Encounter Books, 2002.

A Drawing Activity Involving Transformations

For a change of pace from responding in words to the various situations in this book, we suggest that you have your students do some drawing. First, distribute the handout on pages 82–83. Have students give some thought to what Nick might look like if he were not a teenage boy. Then have them draw Nick as they see him for each question. They can refer to books, magazines, or anything else to guide them in depicting Nick as a vehicle, geometric figure, cat, and so on. You might note especially if Nick is rendered sympathetically in some of the drawings and who the creators of those drawings are.

ACTIVITY

Nick: An Activity Involving Transformations

Morphing Nick

You have certain impressions of Nick after reading the story about him. Here is a chance to put those impressions in pictures. What would he be like in other forms? In each case, on another sheet of paper, draw a picture of what Nick might look like. On the lines below, jot some short descriptions.

1. If Nick were a cat, what would he be like?

_____

_____

2. If Nick were a dog, what breed would he be?

_____

_____

ACTIVITY

Name **Date**

3. If Nick were a tree, what kind would he be?

_____

_____

4. If Nick were a boat, what kind would he be?

_____

_____

5. If Nick were a building, what would he look like?

_____

_____

6. If Nick were a vehicle, what kind would he be?

_____

_____

7. If Nick were a geometric figure, which one would he be?

_____

_____

Hats Off!

Marcus and Ryan were big football fans, especially of the local college team. It was a member of a strong conference; and, when other colleges came to town for a game, the games were important to most of the townspeople.

One Saturday afternoon in September, Ryan suggested that Marcus accompany him to a game. The weather was still very good, and, even though they couldn't afford the best seats, the boys were able to sit along the ten-yard line.

Ryan and Marcus arrived a little late, just as the color guard marched out to display the flag at the center of the field, before the band played the national anthem. As the crowd rose to its collective feet, Marcus removed his cap. The band started to play, and suddenly Ryan's hat flew off his head. He quickly picked it up, realizing that someone behind him had knocked it from his head.

RESPONSES

Name

Date

Hats Off!: Student Responses

Think about your answers to the following questions and write your response to each.

1. Why did someone knock Ryan's hat off his head?

_____

_____

_____

2. How would you have reacted if you were Ryan?

_____

_____

_____

3. Why do people remove their hats when a flag comes by in a parade?

_____

_____

_____

4. What are some other outward signs that we have respect for our country?

_____

_____

_____

Hats Off!:
Respect for One's Country

The Story

Patriotism is a difficult subject to deal with in some classrooms. In others, it is easy. It depends on where the classroom is. Except for anarchists and people whose religious convictions make them believe that saluting the flag is wrong, most people believe it is natural and right to love one's country and to show it. This can be an emotional issue, especially during political campaigns. We have presented a simple (and true) story of a boy's forgetting about the custom requiring people to uncover their heads when the national anthem is played. It is only a custom, of course, and not a law.

You might bring up the controversy that arose in 1996 when a National Basketball Association star, Mahmoud Abdul-Rauf, refused to stand at attention when the national anthem was played at games played by his team, the Denver Nuggets. Abdul-Rauf would stretch while sitting on the bench or stay in the dressing room during the playing of "The Star-Spangled Banner." He was suspended by the league because the NBA requires all of its players to "line up in a dignified posture" for the anthem. Abdul-Rauf asserted that the anthem was a symbol of oppression and tyranny and that the Koran forbids nationalistic ritualism. Muslim officials, however, refuted his claim, saying that "according to Islamic teachings, you worship no one but God, but you respect the flag—you must distinguish between worship and respect." After several days of being suspended, Abdul-Rauf relented and stood with his teammates during the playing of "The Star-Spangled Banner."

The Questions

A few of your students may be genuinely puzzled by reading that someone had knocked Ryan's hat off his head. In certain places the custom is either not uniformly observed or isn't very important. In other places there is more stress placed on outward expressions of patriotism.

Almost any young person would be embarrassed if he or she were Ryan and had a stranger knock off his or her hat. It's insulting, and it could cause an angry reaction.

People remove their hats at various times to show respect. One time is when the flag is paraded, and another is at a funeral.

Three of the other outward signs of respect for our country are pledging allegiance, saluting the flag (putting a hand over the heart is an alternative), and singing the national anthem. The manner in which "The Star-Spangled Banner" is sung by celebrities at athletic contests has also become a topic of debate. Traditionalists have a difficult time accepting the tortured renditions. Your students may also bring up instances when the flag has been burned on our soil or on foreign soil.

An Exercise about Patriotism

To follow up the discussion, administer an exercise such as the one on pages 88–89. Modify it if you think changes can make the exercise more effective with your students. A discussion after the exercise will give you a good idea of how your students interpret the concept of patriotism.

ACTIVITY

Name   Date

Hats Off!: An Activity about Patriotism

Waving the Flag

People have many ways of showing their love of their country. Some of these ways are quite noticeable, and some aren't. Occasionally someone makes a big show of being patriotic, but is that person really acting in his or her own self-interest? Examine each of these behaviors and decide which ones are most patriotic and which are least by ranking them. A rank of 1 is most patriotic, while 12 is least patriotic.

Rankings

_____ Enlisting in the armed forces in time of war

_____ Enlisting in the armed forces in time of peace

_____ Saluting the flag when it is displayed in a parade

_____ Singing "The Star-Spangled Banner" at a game

Name   **Date**

_____ Volunteering to work for the United Way

_____ Voting on all the issues and for the candidates in an election

_____ Obeying the traffic laws

_____ Buying U.S. products instead of foreign products

_____ Wearing red, white, and blue ties

_____ Visiting Washington, DC, and seeing the Lincoln Memorial

_____ Spending a day with others cleaning up the beach

_____ Going to war movies that feature John Wayne

Warm Water

Language arts wasn't their favorite subject, but on this Monday at least both Matt and Ryan, sitting in front, were awake. Mr. Mitchell had a little gleam in his eye that day, which was rather unusual.

"My son Terry is an impatient boy," announced Mr. Mitchell, "and last Saturday, when he was hanging around the mailbox for a kit to arrive, I thought he was going to have a fit."

The class perked up a little at this piece of information. Mr. Mitchell had never before talked about his family.

"I called over to him: 'A watched pot never boils, Terry.' He looked at me as if I were speaking a foreign language. I suppose he'd never heard the expression. Have you? What does it mean?"

Ryan raised his hand and said, "I've never heard that one, either. What *does* it mean? Did you say 'washed pot'? I hate washing the dishes!"

The class laughed at Ryan. Matt pushed him on the shoulder.

"No, Ryan. I said '*watched* pot'—it's watched. But I bet you can figure out what the expression means."

"Oh," muttered Ryan. "A *watched* pot. Someone watches it."

"That's right," said Mr. Mitchell. "You're on the right track. Why is someone watching the pot?"

"Does he want it to boil?" asked Ryan.

"Yes, that's the idea," replied Mr. Mitchell.

"And because he's watching it, the pot doesn't seem to want to boil," reasoned Ryan.

"Exactly, Ryan. So what does the expression mean?"

"It means that as long as Terry kept watching the pot, or the mailbox, his kit wasn't going to arrive," Ryan said.

"Right. That's just what I was telling him when I used that expression. Do you think he took my advice?" asked Mr. Mitchell.

"Nope," Matt said, without raising his hand.

"You're right, Matt. He stuck around the mailbox for another hour before the mail came."

Name   Date

Warm Water: Student Responses

Think about your answers to the following questions and write your
response to each.

1. Have you ever heard that expression? Does anyone in your
family say it?

_____

_____

2. Why did Mr. Mitchell tell the story about his son waiting for the
mail to arrive?

_____

_____

3. Do you think Mr. Mitchell should have asked other students about
the watched pot and not stayed with Ryan? Why or why not?

_____

_____

4. What kind of respect did Mr. Mitchell show in his exchange with Ryan?

_____

_____

Warm Water:
Respect for the Abilities of Others

The Story

Mr. Mitchell was careful not to embarrass Ryan by being patient with him and staying with him instead of switching to another student and getting a quick and correct answer. Getting most of the class to increase their understanding is important, but it is also important to allow students to retain their dignity—that's vitally important to their self-respect. Ryan had the intellectual ability to get the idea of the strange (to him) saying, and Mr. Mitchell gave him credit for having that ability.

The Questions

Many sayings seem almost immortal. They go on and on from generation to generation, even from century to century. It's only when we use an expression and draw blank or puzzled looks from young people that we realize that they have to acquire our treasury of sayings one at a time. So Terry didn't understand about pots boiling (the confusions about metaphors and proverbs are the basis for a large segment of our humor concerning children), and Mr. Mitchell was amused by his son's blank expression.

Mr. Mitchell probably told the story because he's an English teacher and he is interested in language. It was an opportunity, at least in his mind, to teach something about adages. We hope your students appreciate that Mr. Mitchell acted as an experienced teacher should and gave Ryan a chance to come up with the right answer.

The respect Mr. Mitchell showed for Ryan is most admirable. Many teachers take wrong answers and mistaken notions from children and guide those children into coming up with better answers, thereby giving them a better understanding of the subject.

An Activity about the Meaning of Respect

You can follow up the discussion with the exercise on pages 94–95, which is designed to provoke your students into thinking deeply about respect and disrespect. All but three of the statements are "unreasonable," but you and your students may feel otherwise.

ACTIVITY

_____   _____
            Name   Date

Warm Water: An Activity About the Meaning of Respect

What Is Respect?

Place an **S** to the left of the statements you believe to be sensible. Place a **U** to the left of those statements that you think are unreasonable. Think carefully about how the elements in each proposition relate to one another.

_____   **1.** Because Mr. Gonther is fair and broad-minded, his son must also be fair and broad-minded.

_____   **2.** If a person addresses you with a "Mr.," "Miss," or "Ms." before your last name, that person is according you respect.

_____   **3.** When you lie, you are showing disrespect.

Name   **Date**

_____ **4.** A family that has one member who is a bigot should be denied membership in any church, synagogue, or other religious organization.

_____ **5.** If a person tells an ethnic joke, that person is prejudiced.

_____ **6.** If a person enjoys hearing an ethnic joke, that person is prejudiced.

_____ **7.** If you listen to a radio talk show that features people who hate groups of other people, you are therefore endorsing those views.

_____ **8.** Motorists who swear at other motorists in traffic should be apprehended and fined.

_____ **9.** Embezzling and stealing are forms of disrespect.

_____ **10.** Vegetarians demonstrate a profound respect for life.

Threatening a Friendship

Christina invited Becky over to her house after school one day. Knowing Becky was crazy about dancing, Christina wanted to have her see some old Fred Astaire-Ginger Rogers videos that her parents had rented. Christina was a popular girl, partly because she also was good-hearted to almost everyone.

When Christina greeted Becky at the door, she quickly invited her into the living room and offered her a soda. After a while the girls drifted into Christina's bedroom, where there was a television and VCR. Christina was about to play a video when someone rang the doorbell.

"I'll be right back, Becky," called Christina as she ran to the door.

"Okay, Christina, but don't hurry," said Becky.

The person at the front door was a salesman, and Christina didn't know how to get rid of him, so she didn't come right back.

"Christina sure is taking a long time," thought Becky. "Her mother is always telling mine how neat she is. I can still hear someone talking out there. I think I'll find out just how neat Christina really is."

Becky opened a dresser drawer. It was full of nicely folded blouses. Then she quickly closed it and opened the drawer below it. She let out a little gasp. Becky had seen something Christina wouldn't have wanted her to see.

Name

Date

Threatening a Friendship: Student Responses

Think about your answers to the following questions and write your response to each.

1. Becky didn't get caught looking into Christina's dresser drawers, but, if she had been caught, do you think she should have lost a friend? Why or why not?

_____

_____

_____

_____

2. What might have happened if she had been caught?

_____

_____

_____

_____

3. Becky behaved badly. She invaded Christina's privacy. Would you also call what she did a violation of trust? Explain.

_____

_____

_____

_____

For the Teacher

Threatening a Friendship:
Respect for the Privacy of Others

The Story

According to "Miss Manners" and others, people have been known to peek into drawers and closets out of an overwhelming feeling of curiosity. This story isn't far-fetched, then. It says something about temptation, manners, trust, and respect for privacy. Individuals vary greatly in their codes for violating and not violating certain privacies. The really personal privacies are generally regarded in our culture as off-limits. Most people feel very uncomfortable when they accidentally violate them.

The Questions

Your students probably will be divided in their opinions about whether getting caught snooping would end the friendship. After they have given sufficient thought to that question, ask your students for other examples of violating someone's privacy. Here are some:

- Opening another's mail

- Intruding when someone wants to be left alone or when two people want to be left alone

- Being a peeping Tom

- Looking into personal data files

- Reading over someone's shoulder when that person doesn't want you to

- Eavesdropping

- Physical invasions of an individual's body (as in molestation)

If Becky had been caught going through Christina's drawers, Christina could have been irate and might have ordered Becky out of the house. If Christina had not been terribly disturbed, Becky might have offered some lame excuse, and the incident could have been more or less dismissed.

The third question brings up the relationship between trust and honoring someone's privacy. In a real sense, trust is implicit in almost all situations in which privacy is meant to be maintained. Maybe your students can think of a situation when it is not involved in privacy.

A Role-play Activity

After reading the story about Becky and Christina, a role-playing session might reinforce some of the points brought out by the discussion and might uncover others. Select two girls to play Christina and Becky, or ask for two volunteers. The girls can reenact the scene when Christina discovers Becky, and they can reveal their thoughts and emotions to the class. Class members can ask questions of the role-players.

One technique that is often effective in following the role-playing and discussion is providing one of the actors with a double. Place the double beside one of the actors. The double interacts with that actor, bringing out the actor's "other self" and helping her achieve a new level of understanding. The interaction of actor and double often results in new insights.

Maple Leaves Forever

Oh, that's going to be awful . . . hideous!" exclaimed Becky. "I couldn't agree with you more," stated Tanya, frowning and wrinkling her nose.

"If those silver maples are cut down, the nicest thing about this school will be gone," Becky continued. "I don't see how the school board can even consider it. They want to kill those beautiful trees. That's criminal!"

Although additional parking space was undoubtedly needed because of their school's increased enrollment—the teachers, secretaries, and custodians complained that there was no place to park—Becky and Tanya believed that a new parking lot shouldn't mean that a dozen fifty-year-old maples should be cut down. In fact, they were going to fight to save the trees. Together with some of their friends, Tanya and Becky got up a petition to the school board to relocate the new parking lot. They were able to get 253 signatures on the petition in time for the next board meeting, and they were put on the meeting's agenda—right at the beginning.

Seventy-five adults and students showed up at the meeting in support of an alternate plan for parking, which was devised by Tanya's uncle, a landscape architect, and a committee of patrons and students. The president of the school board was taken aback.

"I see you've done your homework," Mr. Graves, the president, said to Becky and Tanya. They had stepped forward to jointly hand in the petition and submit the new plan. "Uh, you certainly have a good deal of support for your position. Our own committee will have to study this plan, of course. At first glance, it does look like a feasible alternative."

Becky, Tanya, and their friends were delighted when the school board accepted the new parking plan a week later, thereby saving the maples.

"You know, Tanya," remarked Becky when they received news of the board's decision, "I think we wouldn't have had the idea to try to save those trees if Mr. Schumacher hadn't told us about those kids who went to their state representative and helped him write a law protecting the covered bridges in Oregon."

RESPONSES

_____
Name

_____
Date

Maple Leaves Forever: Student Responses

Think about your answers to the following questions and write your response to each.

1. Have any young people in your community become involved in issues such as the removal of trees on streets, dangerous intersections, polluted streams, and bicycle paths? If so, describe what they have done.

_____

_____

_____

2. Could a group of students from your school make a presentation to the school board? Why or why not? If you think that it couldn't happen, find out if you are right.

_____

_____

_____

3. In general, do you think younger people are more aware of their surroundings? Are they more disgusted with ugliness than are older people? Explain why you think so.

_____

_____

_____

4. Do you feel a lot better when you are surrounded by beauty? Or does it matter much to you whether your surroundings are especially attractive? Explain.

_____

_____

_____

Maple Leaves Forever:
Respect for Beauty

The Story

Today there are more instances of young people becoming involved in civic issues than ever before. One of the main reasons that this is so can be found in the increasing number of teachers who believe young people can be a force for improving their own lives and the lives of others. The Mr. Schumacher mentioned at the end of the story is typical of many teachers who now encourage their students to become directly involved in the processes of government. For example, an eighth-grade teacher, Alan Haskivitz of Walnut, California, has encouraged his students to host candidate nights, serve as community historians, fingerprint children at local fairs, and lobby the state legislature about water usage. As an outgrowth of their study of water usage, the students researched and drafted a water conservation bill. Then they lobbied it through the California legislature, thereby saving taxpayers millions of dollars and untold amounts of water.

The Questions

It is becoming less unusual for young people to be activists in their communities; your students might have involved themselves recently in a campaign at school or in the community. Many young people have become quite active in environmental issues. As the story points out, it is important for young people that other youngsters are trying to improve their lives and the lives of others by fighting for various causes.

Theoretically, young people can present their concerns at school board meetings. Our question is whether it is practical or not. Depending upon the attitudes of the school board members, serious consideration of legitimate concerns of students is welcome.

The third question about whether young people are more sensitive to their surroundings is meant to provoke your students into thinking of topics such as urban blight, litter, and graffiti. Generally speaking, young people look with "fresher" eyes, whereas older people become more habituated to their surroundings.

Psychologists tell us that all of us, including children, are affected by our surroundings. Some years ago there was a new movement to get away from institutional colors for school buildings. It has also been considered wise policy to plant trees, flowers, and shrubs wherever feasible in shopping malls in order to avoid austerity and add beauty. We are affected, positively and negatively, by the colors, smells, sounds, and sights that assault our senses.

For the Teacher

Students Reviewing Their Surroundings

An obvious follow-up activity for "Maple Leaves Forever" is to have your students survey the school campus's aesthetic features. You don't have to suggest that they find out what should be improved and then try to improve it. That should come from them. You can simply ask for an assessment of the grounds and building(s) with regard to (1) safety, (2) livability, (3) beauty, and (4) relationship to learning. The question of whether the school environment is conducive to learning really encompasses the other three matters. Committees investigating the various factors might spend as little as two days or as much as a month gathering and analyzing information and reporting their findings.

For the Teacher

No Fishing Today

Matt's father had been promising him for weeks that they would hitch up the boat trailer to the pickup and drive to the coast to go salmon fishing. It was getting late in the season, and Matt was an enthusiastic fisherman. Finally, on Friday, Matt's dad told him that the next day was clear on his calendar and that they would tow their boat to a favorite launching spot where the river empties into the ocean.

"The weather report says the conditions are okay, Matt, but there is a storm out on the ocean somewhere. It may take a couple of days for the storm to get to the coast."

Leaving at 4:30 the next morning, the two drove to the place where they usually launched the boat. It was raining, but not too hard.

"I'd better check on the weather again," Matt's father said as he tuned in the pickup's radio to a local station.

"Uh-oh!" he said after hearing a report that the storm was bigger and stronger than had previously been reported. There was a small craft warning in effect and the Coast Guard would probably be telling boats not to cross the bar where the river meets the sea.

"We'd better sit tight until we can learn more about what this storm is doing," said Matt's father.

Matt was terribly disappointed. "Don't you think we can get out there, Dad? We've done it before," he pleaded.

"You don't want to take any chances out on the ocean, Matt. You know that," his father replied.

After four hours of waiting in a nearby restaurant, Matt and his father learned that conditions were not getting any better, and they sadly headed back home.

Name _____ **Date** _____

No Fishing Today: Student Responses

Think about your answers to the following questions and write your
response to each.

1.   There isn't any question that Matt's father was exercising caution in
turning back and going home, but he never did hear that boats were not
allowed to cross the bar on that Saturday. Was he being too cautious,
especially because Matt had been waiting to go fishing for many weeks?

_____

_____

_____

_____

2.   Just what kinds of trouble can small fishing boats get into within
sight of land?

_____

_____

_____

3.   Have you read recent accounts of people being rescued by the Coast
Guard? If so, what were the circumstances?

_____

_____

_____

No Fishing Today:
Respect for the Forces of Nature

The Story
There is a good chance that some of your students will identify with Matt in his disappointment about the aborted fishing adventure. Others will certainly recognize that there are times when all of us have to abandon our plans for reasons of safety, economics, or conflicts. After they have read the story, you can point out that life is full of such disappointments and invite your students to share their experiences.

The Questions
One of the Coast Guard's biggest jobs is rescuing people on pleasure boats when they have gotten into trouble on the ocean. There always seem to be people who take chances, who don't know how to operate their boats properly, who don't have the right equipment, or who are just unlucky with the weather.

An Activity about Respecting the Forces of Nature
The basic elements of air, water, earth, and fire are all to be welcomed—and feared—by people. In recent years all four have been the agents of disaster in California, where earthquakes, forest fires, avalanches, landslides, and floods have ravaged the Golden State. In spite of these disasters, people still greatly underrate the terrible dangers imminent when there is too much wind, rain, or snow. For example, they build homes at the edge of cliffs and rivers and along earthquake fault lines. In Hawaii, they even build villages on the edges of active volcanoes. Although people in many parts of the country ignore the possibility of an earthquake, there is virtually no state that is immune from the effects of a quake.

Have your students organize into four groups to do some research into the genuine possibilities of a disaster from the forces of nature.

The groups can be looking into the possibilities in your community of *flooding* (if your community is not near a river, the students can consider a drought), *hurricanes, tornadoes, earthquakes*, and *fires caused by lightning* (there are many more of these than fires caused by people).

Have them tackle these questions:

1. What can be done to protect the community? What defenses does the community have?

2. What precautions are being taken now to protect the community from these natural disasters?

3. What more can and should be done?

A New Dress

Mildred and Hattie were both healthy thirteen-year-olds, but Mildred didn't like outdoor activities, and Hattie was her father's favorite fishing partner. They were very good friends even though Hattie wasn't fond of television and computer games and Mildred had never fished (nor did she ever intend to). They had other interests in common such as music, parties, clothing, and, occasionally, boys.

Even though she couldn't really understand why Hattie liked to go fishing in nearby streams with her dad and two older brothers, Mildred could appreciate Hattie's enjoyment of the out-of-doors on sunny days. She herself didn't venture out much farther than the shopping mall when school wasn't in session, but she realized that fishing gave Hattie an opportunity to be with her family and to have fun.

One Saturday Hattie came over to Mildred's home because it was a rainy day and the fishing season hadn't started yet. She also wanted to see the new dress that Mildred had told her she'd bought last weekend.

"Come on in, Hattie," Mildred greeted her at the door. "I'll show you my dress."

"If it's as nice as you said, I'm sure I'll like it," said Hattie.

"Well, I just hope it looks as good on me as that blue dress looked on you at Carrie's party. You were lucky to find that—and get your mom to let you buy it."

"You're right," replied Hattie. "I was torn between spending my birthday money on a dress or getting that rod I saw at Menninger's, but I guess I can wait for a while to get the rod. Mr. Menninger said he has several of that model."

"Oh. Well, I know you really want that rod, Hattie. I had the same problem deciding on whether I'd get this dress or a new video by The Shakies. You know, the one we saw on television on Wednesday."

"Choices, choices," Hattie said, and both girls laughed.

Name   **Date**

A New Dress: Student Responses

Think about your answers to the following questions and write your response to each.

1. Do you have a friend who has an interest or hobby that you think is a waste of time? Tell about the friend.

_____

_____

_____

2. Does it surprise you that Mildred is healthy but doesn't spend much time out of doors? Why or why not?

_____

_____

_____

3. Each girl seems to tolerate the other girl's pastime, even though she wouldn't herself bother about doing it. Is that because they are just understanding, or is it because they have been taught to be tolerant of differences in others?

_____

_____

_____

4. What is the relationship, if any, of tolerance and respect? Is tolerance just a weak form of respect?

_____

_____

_____

For the Teacher

A New Dress:
Respect for the Tastes of Others

The Story

Some friends are remarkably tolerant of each other's faults, foibles, and tastes. On the other hand, friends must have common interests and similar outlooks, or they won't have much that they can enjoy together. Hattie and Mildred are the understanding kind of friends. "Mildred" wouldn't consider fishing on the banks of a stream, and Hattie wouldn't spend an afternoon playing computer games. Nonetheless, they don't belittle each other's different passions. The experiences they have together listening to music, gossiping, and going to parties will make their friendship stronger.

The Questions

When it comes to likes and dislikes, young people have probably as many as their elders. Sometimes they are harsh in their judgments of each other, but there is also an amazing amount of conformity. There was a time when Hattie's interest in fishing would have been scoffed at by other people as unladylike, but in many ways girls' interests and opportunities have been broadened greatly.

Most people—and certainly all of the health experts—would urge Mildred to exercise regularly. It is not disclosed in the story whether she exercises at home or at school. But we know that there are many girls who are not inclined to take part in outside activities such as soccer, hiking, tennis, cycling, softball, running, swimming, basketball, gymnastics, or volleyball, indoors or outdoors. They sometimes get their exercise shopping or dancing, but they just aren't inclined to exercise vigorously.

The kind of friendship that Hattie and Mildred have may not be so unusual because they do have several interests in common, and they have mutual respect, which should keep their friendship from foundering.

Tolerance is a very weak form of respect. In fact, to tolerate someone or something is to put up with that person or thing. Not a lot of respect is implied. If we think of tolerance as understanding, however, there is probably much more respect involved. You can see an absence of tolerance, just as you can see definite evidence of one person being tolerant of another's ways or mistakes. These are abstract terms, but they are terribly important to young people in their dealings with each other.

An Activity of Considering Tolerance and Intolerance

Ask your students to think of important events that were characterized by tolerance or intolerance. These events can be those of historical significance, such as the Holocaust and the Crusades, or they can be less significant local happenings.

There have been so many wars, many of them supposedly caused by antithetical religious beliefs, that your students will have no trouble citing a great many conflicts. What about instances in which tolerance has saved the day or made life better? Can they find examples of those in history or in current events?

Give your students time to do some investigating and thinking. The form in which they report their findings can vary from a full-fledged written report by individuals to an oral discussion involving the class for a half-hour or so.

The Spring Sermon

I n spring of every year, Mr. Phillips visits the homeroom classes of the eighth graders. His purpose is to chat with them about high school. In an attempt to get them ready to leave his school and be prepared for what they'll experience in high school, he chats for about fifteen minutes about topics such as peer pressure, study habits, relationships with teachers, and drugs.

On one such visit, after he had spent ten minutes or so dealing with several subjects, Mr. Phillips paused and launched into the one that was dearest to his heart.

"Of course, everything I've said you've probably heard before, and you've probably been turning me off even as you look up wide-eyed at me."

"Ain't that the truth!" Leon thought to himself.

"But there is one thing I'm going to say that I hope you'll remember: Think twice before you do something that that little voice inside you says is wrong. Pause, and reflect that you could be involving people other than yourself in what you are about to do. You know right from wrong. If everyone around you is doing something wrong, and you know it is wrong, you don't have to do it too."

Several students looked at each other and smirked. One or two yawned. Leon muttered under his breath, "And I'll bet you've never had any fun, either!"

When class was dismissed, Barry said to Leon: "What a lot of hot air! We've heard all that stuff before."

Leon responded with, "That old geezer gives the same talk every year. My brother James told me about Phillips doing that routine for the eighth graders three years ago. He said it was a laugh."

"Whatever happened to James, Leon? I haven't seen him for a while," Barry asked.

"Oh, he's in a special school now. Had a little trouble with the law. Got unlucky when he made a 'pass' near the high school last fall. The cops got him for dealing," Leon explained.

Name   **Date**

The Spring Sermon: Student Responses

Think about your answers to the following questions and write your response to each.

1. Is Mr. Phillips wasting his time and the time of the eighth graders by giving his little talk every spring? Why do you think so?

_____

_____

_____

2. Have you heard something like Mr. Phillips's talk before? When?

_____

_____

_____

3. What do you think of his advice? Explain.

_____

_____

_____

4. By ignoring what adults have said to him, Leon is dooming himself to learn "the hard way"—by experience. Maybe that's the only way any of us learn the lessons of life. What do you think?

_____

_____

_____

The Spring Sermon:
Respect for Wisdom

The Story

Orienting eighth graders or ninth graders for their matriculation to high school was once more common than it is now. A principal or teacher is more likely to deliver Mr. Phillips's sermon to fifth graders or sixth graders going into middle school or junior high. That this is so is a sad commentary about the fact that young people are exposed to more negative influences at an earlier age than ever before. The "sermon" might be received as cynically in some communities by Barry's and Leon's counterparts in the fifth grade.

The Questions

Evidently, Mr. Phillips believes it is still worth a try to give his little talk to eighth graders, even though he sees a good deal of evidence that he is wasting his breath with many of the students. There might be one or two students, he reasons to himself, who will take his words to heart.

It would be deeply disappointing to us if a good portion of your students say that they haven't heard this advice before. They should have heard it first from their parents.

The third question is designed to force your students to respond to what we really believe is wise advice. Peer pressure seems to be much more powerful than wise advice by adults, however.

Your students are perhaps too young to reflect about how human beings learn, often unhappily, from their unfortunate experiences. It is probably the *only* way many of us ever learn to cope with life's vicissitudes.

For the Teacher

An Exercise about Wisdom

We have an abundance of aphorisms, adages, proverbs, and witty sayings in the English language. Most of these sayings pass for bits of wisdom. Some, however, are contradictory: we have "Look before you leap" and also "He who hesitates is lost." With that pair, you can see that there is a bit of wisdom in both.

Page 119 is a handout with a dozen statements. Distribute it to your students and ask them to decide if each statement is wise, unwise, or debatable. All of the statements have been regarded by some people as wise sayings. Most of them will be familiar to your students. Here are their sources:

1. Familiar saying
2. Confucius
3. Familiar saying
4. Recent familiar saying
5. Familiar saying
6. Benjamin Marcuslin
7. Recent familiar saying
8. Aesop
9. Familiar saying
10. Familiar saying
11. Familiar saying
12. Benjamin Marcuslin

Name   Date

The Spring Sermon: An Activity about Wisdom

Which Are the Wise Ones?

Here are twelve statements that are commonly believed to be gems of wisdom. Which of them can be considered wise, which ones are probably unwise, and which could be either wise or unwise? Circle the number next to the "wise" statements. Put a question mark next to the number of those that could be either wise or unwise.

1. Money is the root of all evil.

2. What you do not wish for yourself, do not do to others.

3. The bigger they are, the harder they fall.

4. If it feels good, do it.

5. Time waits for no one.

6. He that falls in love with himself will have no rivals.

7. Don't trust anybody over forty.

8. Every man tries to convince himself that the thing he can't have is of no value.

9. Cleanliness is next to Godliness.

10. Anything worth doing is worth doing well.

11. Beauty is only skin deep.

12. Little strokes fell great oaks.

Shocked

Tanya ran up to Becky before class began. "Did you hear what happened?" asked Tanya.

"No. What do you mean?" responded Becky.

"Someone drove by the synagogue on Grove Street and shot a hole through the window. I can't believe it could happen in our town. We have a lot of different kinds of people and *all* of the religions," Tanya said, "and there hasn't ever been anything like that before."

"I can't believe it, either, Tanya," Becky declared. "Why would anyone do anything so stupid as that?"

"Well, we've had some peculiar people making some crazy comments lately. They say there's an increase in neo-Nazi activities everywhere in the country. From what I've read about Hitler and the Nazis, it's hard to believe that anyone could buy that nonsense," remarked Tanya.

"What are the police going to do?" asked Becky.

"We'll have to wait and see. The radio said they were 'looking into the incident.' I hope they catch the morons who did it. I'm just wondering how it will affect the people who go to the synagogue this Saturday."

No arrests were made, and some people in the town were saying to each other that at least no one was injured and that the town hadn't had any drive-by shootings before, the kind in which someone is wounded or killed. Nevertheless, a majority of the people were a little shaken. In their town the churches, synagogues, and mosques were special places. To some, they were sacred places. These people felt attacked even though it wasn't their place of worship that was hit.

_____   _____
Name   **Date**

Shocked: Student Responses

Think about your answers to the following questions and write your response to each.

1. Has there been an incident in your town when a church, synagogue, or mosque was vandalized or desecrated in any way?

_____

_____

2. Do you have any group such as the Skinheads or the Ku Klux Klan in your community? Do people in your town regard the hate groups in the United States as oddities or something to really worry about?

_____

_____

_____

_____

3. Places of worship are designed to inspire respect. Maybe that's why we are shocked when someone shows a marked lack of respect for a religious building or service. How do you feel when you enter a place that is meant for worship?

_____

_____

_____

Shocked:
Respect for Places of Worship

The Story

There are elements of both respect and disrespect in this true story. Tanya and Becky indicate that they are shocked by the fact that someone shot out a window in a synagogue, although neither attends services there. That is, they feel everyone should respect such a place. They react the way people usually do when there is an event out of keeping with the character of a person, as happens when a mayor is convicted of using cocaine two days after he has lectured schoolchildren about the evils of drugs.

The Questions

Chances are good that your students are aware of one or more ugly incidents involving race, religion, sexual orientation, age, or gang-based crime. If they are inclined to discuss these incidents, an excellent source for ideas about studying hate crimes is *Respecting Our Differences* by Lynn Duvall. Her book will provide you with a good deal of ammunition (no pun intended) about the topic.

Even if your community is free of hate crimes, the fact that they are on the increase in the country is something to be concerned about. As happened in the sixties to small, relatively trouble-free communities when drug problems occurred elsewhere, it was only a matter of time until those awful problems became local concerns. Teachers and community leaders must be prepared for incursions by groups that spew hate and intolerance.

There are places of worship that inspire awe as well as respect. One thinks of the great cathedrals of Europe, for example. We hope all of your students have experienced that special feeling when entering a house of worship.

References

Duvall, L. *Respecting Our Differences*. Minneapolis, MN: Free Spirit Publishing, 1994.

"How Do You Respond to Religious Intolerance Among Students?" *NEA Today* 22 (February 2004): 44.

An Activity about Liking and Positive Feelings

The best way to modify behavior in a positive direction is to encourage individuals to have pleasant, positive thoughts about others. (Conversely, in time of war there is a lot of attention given to getting people to have negative thoughts about the enemy.) To encourage your students to think "good" thoughts, have them write song lyrics about liking—not loving—others (including animals). If you think the activity will be more successful that way, have your students write the lyrics in a "rap" style. Because popular songs almost always rhyme, they may have an easier time composing their lyrics if they can think of a definite rhythm.

ACTIVITY

Name   Date

Shocked: An Activity about Liking and Positive Feelings

You'd Be So Easy to Like

There is an old and beloved popular song entitled "You'd Be So Easy to Love." Yes, it is an old-fashioned love song, but the lyrics are successful partly because they give the *reasons* why the singer would find it easy to fall in love with a special someone.

Make up a song that tells why it is easy to *like* someone, but give reasons that have nothing to do with romantic love (the kind where people love each other because of looks, charm, or personality). In your song, give reasons why it is easy to like the person or animal. Choose one of the ten people or animals listed below and write song lyrics telling just why it is easy to like them.

- a baby
- a two-month-old puppy
- an eleven-year-old cat
- a grandmother
- a grandfather

- a great athlete
- a person who works very hard
- a police officer
- a very kind person
- a very funny person

ACTIVITY

_____   _____
Name   **Date**

You can write your first draft here:

_____

_____

_____

_____

_____

_____

_____

_____

_____

_____

_____

Wings Versus Wheels

It was Monday morning and the class was discussing a recent airline disaster that took the lives of all the passengers and crew members. Ms. Newman wanted the discussion to proceed to another current events topic because the story really bothered her, but several of her students were reluctant to leave the story of the airplane crash.

Geraldine said, "I don't know how those planes can crash so often when they have all of those instruments—the radar and computers and everything."

"Perhaps we haven't advanced to the stage when we can eliminate the risk in an undertaking so unnatural as flying through the air," commented Ms. Newman.

That stopped the discussion for a moment.

"What do you mean 'unnatural'?" asked Tom.

"Why, we have two legs and two arms, but neither is very well adapted to put us in the air and fly," answered Ms. Newman.

There was another pause, and Ms. Newman was about to proceed to the next current event when Tanya offered: "I believe it's a lot safer to ride a bus than to take an airplane somewhere. Besides, I've heard that airplane pilots make a lot more money than bus drivers do. Is that fair?"

"How do you know they do? Have you seen the statistics?" challenged Ryan.

"I can't remember where I heard that pilots make a lot of money, but I think people should ride the buses more and then bus drivers would get more money," replied Tanya.

Ms. Newman listened carefully during the exchange between Tanya and Ryan. She thought that Tanya was incorrect about the relative safety of flying and taking a bus, but she didn't want to make Tanya look foolish in the eyes of her classmates.

After Ryan had looked at the ceiling and grunted, Ms. Newman smiled and said, "I think Tanya has a point about how much pay bus drivers get. Maybe they should be paid more. Have any of you read anything about airplane fatalities in comparison with other kinds of transportation? I'd really like to know if it is a lot safer to ride a bus rather than to drive or be a passenger in a car or take a plane. Tanya may be right that taking a bus is safer than riding in a car, and if so, bus drivers certainly should be paid well."

Tanya looked pleased, and her classmates seemed satisfied that she had contributed something to the discussion. She didn't often speak up.

RESPONSES

Name   **Date**

Wings Versus Wheels: Student Responses

Think about your answers to the following questions and write your response to each.

1. Do you think Tanya should say taking a bus is safer than taking an airplane without having something to back up her statement?

_____

_____

2. Should Ryan have challenged Tanya? Why or why not?

_____

_____

_____

3. How did Ms. Newman show respect for Tanya?

_____

_____

4. Do you think any of the students followed up and did some research about transportation safety? Why or why not?

_____

_____

_____

5. When does an opinion cease to be an opinion and become a reliable statement?

_____

_____

_____

Wings Versus Wheels:
Respect for the Opinions of Others

The Story

Ms. Newman knew that driving a car is about ten times more dangerous than traveling by plane or train. She actually didn't know if taking a bus is safer than driving an automobile, but she suspected it might be and she wanted to have the students look into the matter of transportation safety and get the answers for themselves. Tanya had some definite opinions, one of which could be wrong, but Ms. Newman was able to open up the discussion a little and spare Tanya any embarrassment.

The Questions

Obviously we all make innumerable statements that we can't back up with facts. If we always had to have some kind of proof for our opinions, we'd be talking a lot less. But in discussions that call for facts or statistics such as the one in Ms. Newman's class, there is a need for some kind of supporting evidence.

We hope most of your students agree that Ryan had a right to question Tanya to determine whether her opinions had some kind of basis in facts.

Ms. Newman, an experienced teacher, felt that if she didn't broaden the discussion a little Tanya could become somewhat hurt, especially if Ryan and others knew she was on shaky ground when she said bus transportation is safer than air transportation. Rather than telling Tanya that the highways are ten times more unsafe than the skyways, she asked her students to find out just how safe transportation is by the three modes of travel.

Some teachers habitually ask their students to "look up" a subject and then never follow up that invitation. In this case, it is likely that Ms. Newman did encourage her students enough to find out about transportation safety (airplane crashes get a lot of attention in the media) and then share their findings with the class.

Because opinions can become factual statements when there is sufficient evidence to support them, we can liken them, somewhat grandly, to untested hypotheses. Mostly, however, opinions reflect insufficient thinking and are subject to continual revision.

For the Teacher

An "Accidental" Exercise about Distinguishing Facts from Opinions

You can sharpen the distinction between a fact and an opinion for your students with the exercise on the next page. Distribute the handout on pages 131–132. Ask students to think about the statements and label each as a fact or opinion. Here are our responses to the six statements.

1. Opinion. It might be true that women are safer drivers, but as the statement stands, it's just an opinion. Things change. The insurance companies can provide the current facts.

2. Fact. It happened in Malaga, Spain.

3. Opinion. With a word such as *probably* in a statement, you don't have a fact. The statement is true, however.

4. Opinion. This is obviously an opinionated statement: The *shouldn't* is a sure indication.

5. Fact. That drunk drivers are more likely to be hurt or killed in a car crash can be verified by recent statistics. Statements such as this one, when provable, are facts.

6. Fact. Those statistics were quoted in 1991, but they are probably still accurate.

For the Teacher

ACTIVITY

Name   **Date**

Wings Versus Wheels: An Activity about Facts and Opinions

Accidentally

Label each of the following statements as either "fact" or "opinion" and tell why you think so.

1. Women are safer drivers than men.

_____

_____

_____

2. According to the National Transportation Safety Board, fifty people who died in a post-crash fire in a DC-10 airplane were sitting in the back of the plane and failed to move up to the next available exit.

_____

_____

_____

ACTIVITY

Name   Date

3. Drivers over fifty years old are probably involved in more side-impact automobile accidents because they have vision problems.

_____

_____

_____

4. Anyone over ninety years old shouldn't be allowed to drive a car.

_____

_____

_____

5. Drunk drivers are more likely to be hurt or killed in a car crash.

_____

_____

_____

6. Each year more than 10,000 Americans are injured and 120 are killed in collisions with animals.

_____

_____

_____

The Big Dance

Looking flustered, Marcus rushed over to Matt in the cafeteria at noon recess.

"What's up, Marcus?" Matt asked.

"I think we have a problem," Marcus blurted out. "There's a nasty rumor going around that all the money we make putting on the dance is going to go for drugs and a party for the club afterward."

"Who'd believe that?" said Matt. "That's idiotic! We don't do things like that!"

"I don't know if anyone will believe it or not, but it might really affect how many people will come to the dance, let alone how a lie like that could spoil our reputations!" Marcus exclaimed angrily.

"Oh, I see Ashley over there. Let's ask her if she's heard that rumor," Matt said.

"Yes, I've heard it. I think we'd better do something about it. Probably Leon is behind that awful talk. Maybe there's time before the dance to put a stop to that. Why doesn't Tom make a statement in the school paper? He's president," said Ashley.

The three found Tom and explained what was happening.

"Okay, I'll ask for space in the paper. It comes out on Wednesday, and the dance is on Saturday night. I'll tell them just what our profits are to be used for—for library equipment, not drugs! I'll go over right now and see Mr. Wilson and Ned Johnson, the editor," promised Tom, and he walked briskly to Mr. Wilson's room.

Tom's statement appeared in the school newspaper, but there wasn't much comment among the students about it. The Dance Club members wondered if anyone would come. An hour after the dance started, Becky got together with Ashley and Christina.

"What a turnout! There's hardly room in the gym for the dancers," Becky said happily.

"I'm sure relieved," Ashley sighed. "I could just see a whole bunch of parents telling their kids not to come because of that rumor about us using the money for drugs. Everyone's here but Leon."

"Oh that Leon! He's just jealous and wants to be mean. Nobody believed him," Christina declared. "The kids know who is telling the truth."

Name

Date

The Big Dance: Student Responses

Think about your answers to the following questions and write your response to each.

1. Have any phony rumors gone around your school lately? If so, what were they?

_____

_____

_____

2. Oftentimes jealousy is the basis for gossip and false rumors. How would you deal with a lie about yourself that was circulating among your classmates because someone is jealous of you?

_____

_____

_____

_____

3. Do you believe that you can usually tell when someone is lying? Do you know when someone is telling the truth? Explain.

_____

_____

_____

_____

The Big Dance:
Respect for Truth

The Story

The big problem with malicious rumors is that they put a question in the minds of the people who hear them that is very difficult to remove. Even though those people might seriously doubt the truth of the rumor, there is still a residue of the rumor left in their minds. The person who is the subject of the false rumor is irrevocably hurt because people remember rumors about mischief and wrongdoing more readily than they recall comments about good deeds. "Where there's smoke, there's fire," someone often says. We feel an outrage when a good person's reputation is damaged by a malicious rumor, but in most cases denials don't completely eradicate the harm done.

The Questions

As young people grow older, they are subject to more and more of the uncharitable motives of their peers. By the time they are in high school, students know firsthand about nasty rumors and innuendoes. This story most likely will provoke some rather strong emotions in your students. If not, they are quite fortunate. We don't have to warn you that, in many classrooms, this unit could ignite some verbal fireworks.

The second question is one of the most important asked in all twenty-five units in this book. When the subject of disrespect is raised, a logical question is: "What can you do about it?" What can a young person do about a lie that is being circulated about her or him? Possible answers would be (1) to deny the lie to everyone, (2) to confront the person spreading the lie, and (3) to ignore the lie and show by one's behavior that it is a lie. Your students may have other strategies.

The last question is a fascinating one because there has always been a debate about whether it is possible to know, with a great deal of assurance, if someone is telling the truth. Unfortunately, this subject is confounded by such matters as whether the person not telling the truth is aware that he or she is misrepresenting the facts and whether the individual is a habitual (pathological) liar who can't distinguish between truth and falsity. We have lie detectors, but it has been shown that they can be deceived; that is, the person administering the test with a lie detector can be fooled. And then there are the philosophers who wonder whether the truths of this world can ever be really known. Your students, however, will probably talk about physical mannerisms as tell-tale clues when someone is prevaricating. Practiced liars, unfortunately, don't give themselves away very often.

An Activity about Truth

A natural outcome of this unit is a serious discussion of the common—and very important—words *fact*, *lie* (*falsehood*), *truth*, and *rumor*. Discuss the intent of the speaker or writer in telling a lie; for example, there are "black" lies and "little white" lies. Many years ago there was a popular song entitled "It's a Sin to Tell a Lie." Is it? If so, is it a major sin or a minor sin? Nearly everyone fails to tell the truth now and then. (Or is it, as some think, all sin, with no judgment of seriousness?)

People and rumors go together. Some serve a good purpose, as when news of a discovery, an important change of some kind, or an impending event serves to alert people about something affecting their lives. Malicious rumors create harm, distrust, and fear; whatever can be done to wipe them out should be done. Playful rumors sometimes aren't so harmless; they may be started in jest, but they can have serious consequences. Your students will have some interesting observations about each of these powerful words.

the forces of nature, 105–108
an individual's worth, 53–57
intellectual property, 9–15
intelligence, 114–119
living things, 58–62
the opinions of others, 126–132
parents, 47–52
the privacy of others, 96–99
the property of others, 36–42
religious beliefs, 120–125
self, 78–83
senior citizens, 16–20
the tastes of others, 109–113
the truth, 133–137
young people, 31–35
respect, mutual. *See* abilities of others, respect for
rudeness, 68–71
    activity, student, 71
    case study, 68–69
    teacher guide, 71
    work sheet, 70
rumors. *See* truth, respect for the

S

self-expression. *See* creative efforts
self, respect for, 78–83
senior citizens, respect for, 16–20

T

teacher guides
    ability of others, respect for, 93
    altruism, 19–20
    authority, respect for, 75
    beauty, respect for, 103–104
    confidence, lack of, 80–81
    courtesy, 45
    creative thinking, 23–24
    cultural differences, 28–30
    discrimination against young people, 33
    harassment, 56–57, 66–67
    honesty, 39–40
    ideas, different, 7–8
    intelligence, respect for, 117–118
    intolerance, 112–113
    nature, respect for the forces of, 108
    opinions of others, respect for, 129–130

patriotism, 86–87
plagiarism, 12–13
privacy of others, respect for, 98–99
religious beliefs, respect for, 123
respect for living things, 61–62
respect for parents, 50
rudeness, 71
truth, respect for the, 136–137
temper tantrums, 47–48, 50
tolerance. *See* intolerance
Torrance's Incomplete Figures Test, 23
truth, respect for the, 133–137
    activity, student, 137
    case study, 133–134
    teacher guide, 136–137
    work sheet, 135

W–X–Y

wisdom, respect for. *See* intelligence, respect for
work sheets
    abilities of others, respect for, 92
    altruism, 18
    authority, respect for, 74
    beauty, respect for, 102
    confidence, lack of, 79
    courtesy, 44
    creative thinking, 22
    cultural differences, 27
    discrimination, 32
    harassment, 55, 65
    honesty, 38
    ideas, different, 6
    intelligence, respect for, 116
    intolerance, 111
    nature, respect for the forces of, 107
    opinions of others, respect for, 128
    patriotism, 85
    plagiarism, 11
    privacy of others, respect for, 97
    religious beliefs, respect for, 122
    respect for living things, 60
    respect for parents, 49
    rudeness, 70
    truth, respect for the, 135
worship. *See* religious beliefs
young people, respect for, 31–35